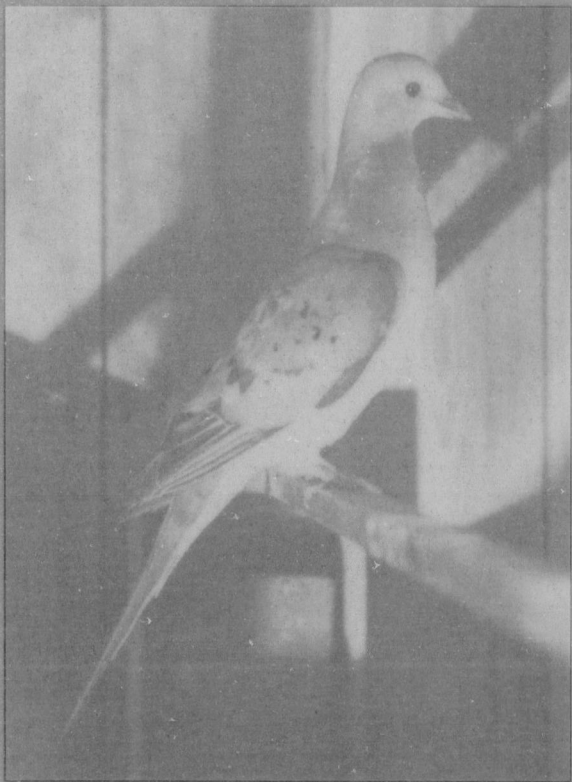

ANTHROPOSCENES   ANTHROPOSCENITIES

Suppose there is a pigeon, suppose there is.
GERTRUDE STEIN, TENDER BUTTONS, 1914

Female Passenger Pigeon (*Ectopistes migratorius*) 1898,
16 years before extinction of entire species. The last one, her
keepers named Martha, died 1914, at the Cincinnati Zoo.
(nous sommes tous des pigeons migrateurs)

THE SUPPOSIUM

Thought Experiments & Poethical Play in Difficult Times

BEYOND DEFAULT GEOMETRIES OF ATTENTION

> You'll agree that there is more than one kind of poetry
> in the true sense of the word—that is to say, calling
> something into existence that was not there before.

DIOTIMA TO SOCRATES, PLATO'S *SYMPOSIUM*

Black Dada is a way to talk about
the future while talking about the past

ADAM PENDLETON, *BLACK DADA*

ISBN: 978-1-933959-31-3

Cover art by Joan Retallack
Design and typesetting by HR Hegnauer

Cover images:
"Passenger Pigeon: Profile View with Shadow," J.G. Hubbard, 1896. Image #32610 courtesy
    Wisconsin Historical Society.
The University of Western Australia Archives 50764P – *Diotima*, Victor Wager, 1937, Portland
    stone, The University of Western Australia Art Collection, Gift of Professor Whitfeld, 1936.
Thales' Foot, "The Astrologer Who Fell into A Well," John Tenniel illustration for *Aesop's
    Fables*, 1884. Public Domain.
Miles Davis performing live onstage at Newport Jazz Festival, photo © 1967, David Redfern,
    Redferns Collection, Getty Images. Permission courtesy of the Miles Davis Estate.
"Yellow Jacket," Beverly Semmes, ink on magazine page, 2013. Image courtesy of the artist
    and Susan Inglett Gallery, New York, NY.
Fawaar Refugee Camp plaza. Photo courtesy of Campus in Camps.

Litmus Press is a program of Ether Sea Projects, Inc., a 501(c)(3) non-profit literature and arts
organization. Dedicated to supporting innovative, cross-genre writing, the press publishes the
work of translators, poets, and other writers, and organizes public events in their support. We
encourage interaction between poets and visual artists by featuring contemporary artworks
on the covers of our books. By actualizing the potential linguistic, cultural, and political
benefits of international literary exchange, we aim to ensure that our poetic communities
remain open-minded and vital.

This book is made possible by the Leslie Scalapino – O Books Fund, individual
members and donors. All contributions are fully tax-deductible.

Cataloging-in-publication data is available from the Library of Congress.

Litmus Press   Small Press Distribution
925 Bergen Street, Suite 405   1341 Seventh Street
Brooklyn, New York 11238   Berkeley, California 94710
litmuspress.org   spdbooks.org

CONTENTS

IV
SUPPOSIUM 2014, DOCUMENTATION

V

VI

JOAN RETALLACK

The Wager

THOUGHT EXPERIMENTS, POETHICAL PLAY, DIFFICULT TIMES

"Supposium" is said to have 2 to 4 stable isotopes that do not decay into other elements. It may or may not be radioactive. If radioactive, its half-life is too long to be measured. Supposium is currently found in the sub-terrain of chemistry textbooks, periodically accessed for mostly benign thought experiments. Neither obviously utopian nor blatantly dystopian, the Supposium thought experiment awaits further analysis to determine long-term implications. S.M. QUANT

During the conversation when Adam Pendleton invited me to propose a contribution to his 2013–14 artist residency at MoMA, Plato's account of Socrates and friends enjoying their debate on *erōs* in the *Symposium* (c. 370 BCE) came to mind. Supposium (2014 CE) materialized as homage and play on what I have taken to be the *Symposium*'s most fascinating aspect—a startling departure from the default masculine supremacy of the misogynist classical world and its philosophical patriarchy. I'm referring to the feminine swerve that the sudden appearance of poet-philosopher-priestess Diotima of Mantinea represents, and goes on to enact, after Socrates introduces her, without irony, as wise in many things but, apropos the occasion, his mentor on the nature of love. Socrates (whom I've come to think of as Plato's feminine alter-ego) is not speaking of Diotima's expertise on sexual assignation, but of her thoughtful analysis of *erōs* as the moving principle of *philosophia*, love of wisdom: the passion for truth, justice, and intellectual argument. Diotima, in fact, excels at arguing; not surprisingly, in the Socratic manner that—wily, seductive, relentless—can address matters of utmost gravitas by means of playful thought experiments.

When I refer to Diotima as "feminine swerve," I'm thinking of what Lucretius explains (c. 50 BCE) to his Roman readers in the Epicurean poem, *De Rerum Natura* (*On the Nature of Things*):

> One further point in this matter I desire you to understand: that while the elements are being carried downward by their own weight in a straight line through the void, at times indeterminate and in indeterminate places, they swerve a little from their course, just so much as you might call a slight change of motion. For if they were not apt to incline, all would fall forever downward like raindrops into the profound void, no element striking any other: and so nature would never have produced anything.

For Epicurus (c. 341–270 BCE), the swerve was a matter of metaphysics beyond human control. Like most philosophers in the turbulent ancient world, parsing what is and is not within our control was a paramount task of setting out both reassurances and limits to our desires and intentions. (Retrospectively, Epicurus via Lucretius can be seen as foreshadowing Darwin's chance mutations.) The human, ethical challenge (Epicurus's chief interest was justice and compassion among ordinary people in everyday life) remains much the same—to use our wits and creativity to swerve ourselves out of the profound void of default sociopolitical patterns perpetuating misogyny, racism, fear and hatred of alterity of all kinds, despoiling our (all species included) Earth. Might bold thought experiments and poethical play create imaginative climates that can generate consequential swerves? Just as out-of-the-blue atmospheric disturbances generate both thrilling and calamitous storms, there are risks. In the case of thought experiments beckoning swerves the worst outcome is probably boredom. Not to minimize that. As La Rochefoucauld pointed out (c. 1665), we can forgive those who bore us, but not those whom we bore.

Suppose a curated event, billing itself as a series of invited thought experiments beginning with *suppose*, is procedurally designed to experiment with the structure of the event itself in such a way that everyone present becomes increasingly drawn from periphery to center. (See Sandi Hilal's thought experiment for sociopolitical implications of this geometrical shift.) The *modus operandi* for SUPPOSIUM

2014 was to set this experiment ticking somewhere inside MoMA—ideally placed in implicit dialogue with the structural *habitus* of the museum. *Habitus,* in Pierre Bourdieu's sense of a largely unconscious, self-perpetuating value framework that tends to cordon off threats to its perpetual reinscription. The idea was that as the event went on implications and consequences of language used in the opening presentations would be reflected upon, altered and/or magnified by an audience gradually morphing into participants.

In its simplest construction, SUPPOSIUM 2014 turned out to be a peaceful takeover of the MoMA Founders Room. Peaceful but laborious. A labor of furniture moving that, retrospectively, should have been (had MoMA's insurance allowed it) part of the public event. Immense, dark-stained tables, hefty executive-upholstered chairs (enough to seat about forty important people) had to be hidden away in another part of the building. Emptied of its material gravitas the room turned out to be large enough for approximately 125 people to engage in a variety of peripatetic workshop groups, capped by self-organized performative play. Successive rearrangements of lightweight movable chairs allowed reconfigurations from rows to circles to a room-sized oval whose center, shaped like a giant paramecium, became the performance space.

From the start we had activated a procedure that would turn into a card game (using index cards) called *SWERVED.* As people arrived they found game kits set out on every chair: 4"×6" spiral pads (red, yellow, or blue), index cards, pen, instructions for deployment. Prior to the speakers' thought experiments opening the supposium, everyone was asked to engage in active listening by writing down striking words and phrases for later use. (Focus on words was in recognition of their power to redirect geometries of attention.) Culled language, along with reflective notes, entered the composition of nine group performances and was ultimately recomposed—using a simple alphabetical procedure—into the collaborative poem *SWERVED* that ends this book.

Section I presents texts of five invited thought experiments as delivered in the MoMA Founders Room on March 2, 2014. Sections II and III contain contributions by audience participants written in aftermath of the event. (*Aftermath*, etymological roots: new grass springing up after [Germanic dialect] *math*/mowing.) All audience participants were invited to submit work in any medium or genre for the book.

The documentation section contains material generated during the lead up to the supposium: invitations, links with a John Cage exhibition coinciding in the museum with the supposium, the event introduction, and two subsequent reviews. It might in fact be useful to look through that section to more fully contextualize the origin of the initial thought experiments. The complete text of the procedurally composed poem *SWERVED*, with contributions from almost all of the participants, has pride of place as a non-concluding culmination.

BIBLIOGRAPHY

La Rochefoucauld. *Réflexions ou sentences et maximes morales.* Paris: Éditions Garnier Frères, 1961.

Lucretius. *De Rerum Natura / On the Nature of Things.* Translated by W.H.D. Rouse and revised by Martin Ferguson Smith. Cambridge MA & London: Harvard University Press, 1992.

Plato. *Symposium.* Translated by Alexander Nehamas and Paul Woodruff. Indianapolis & Cambridge: Hackett Publishing Co, 1989.

Quant, S.M. *Manual for Desperate Times.* Washington D.C. and Paris: Pre-Post-Eros Editions, frothcoming.

THE SUPPOSIUM

I

THOUGHT EXPERIMENTS BEGINNING WITH

SUPPOSE

SANDI HILAL

Decolonizing Architecture: Merging Public and Private in Fawaar Refugee Camp

Suppose the UN General Assembly had the power to implement Resolution 194, which declares the right for Palestinian refugees to return home. What would happen to the Palestinian refugee camp as it exists today? From where would the refugees leave and where exactly would they go? In order to answer such questions, I will first look at the history of the camps, going back to 1948 when Palestinians forced to leave their homes, villages, and cities in what is today's Israel became refugees.

As they were leaving—escaping—spaces zoned as refugee camps were established, with tents distributed to families. The Palestinian refugees lived in these tents for a while but, as winter came, they began to build homes. But a problem arose: soon after constructing the four walls they had to face the question of whether to build the roof. What did it mean for refugees back then to build a roof? What implications did building a roof have for the right of return? Would building roofs mean they were accepting that this was no longer a temporary shelter situation? Early on Palestinian refugees decided not to build the roofs. That meant they had decided not to settle in these camps. Their strategy to guarantee return to their homes would be to build a temporary, roofless camp so the international community would recognize them as vulnerable refugees (without even a roof over their heads)—people who clearly needed to be allowed to return to their homes.

Well, sixty-five years have passed since the decision to build a roofless camp, and if you visit a camp today you will find a very different reality. In the case of Deheishe refugee camp, in less than half a square kilometer you have more than forty NGOs, you have swimming pools, you have libraries and multistory houses. You will not even recognize it as a camp. But when you naively ask them why they are building a swimming pool in a refugee camp, their answer is that they will destroy the swimming pool immediately and even the whole camp if this means that they will return home.

However, what does it mean to destroy sixty-five years of exile, what does it mean to erase the camp from the narration of the return? What does it mean to decide that to return to their homes they should have a tabula rasa? These are all questions that we are trying to work on, and one of the main issues is that of how to bring the right of return back into the narration of the camp itself—how the camp can become a central part of what we are doing when we are narrating the right of return. So far, the camp has been erased from the narration of the right of return. The question now is not only how to bring it back but also to understand what it means *today* to be a refugee living in a refugee camp.

> Refugee camps are sites where neither public nor private property exists. After sixty-four years, Palestinian refugees still cannot legally own their own houses (though in practice they do). The camp is a space carved from the occupied territorial state. Though states and nongovernmental organizations actively participate in conceptualizing and managing the camps, we are still struggling to fully comprehend the camp-form. How that form has contaminated and radically transformed the reality of the city as an organized and functional political community. Thus, the birth of the camp calls into question the very idea of the city as a democratic space. If the political representation of a citizen is to be found in public space, in the camp we find its inverse: here, a citizen is stripped of his or her political rights. In this sense, the camp represents a sort of anti-city, but also a potential counter-site in which a new form of urbanism is emerging beyond the idea of the nation-state.[1]

> One of the only kinds of common lands that survived in Palestine in face of colonial domination is called Al-mashaa'. It derives from customary

---

1 Alessandro Petti and Sandi Hilal, "BEYOND THE PUBLIC: A COMMON SPACE IN FAWAAR REFUGEE CAMP," *Theatrum Mundi*, March 4, 2013.

practices and refers to land collectively owned by different farmers. Israeli authorities, suspicious of this form of ownership that hovers between private and public, have declared Al-mashaa' as state land and have taken control of it.[2]

However, I like to look at refugee camps as one of the remaining places in Palestine where a form of life in collectivity still exists. In order to tell the story of the common in the camp I would like to tell the story of a plaza in one of the southern refugee camps in the West Bank. And by telling the story of this project I would like to expand on the notion of *Al-mashaa'*, because I think that will help us to understand better how to bring the right of return back into the narration of the camp. I think it can be done by reactivating the form of collectivity of *Al-mashaa'*.

In May 2008, in the Fawaar Refugee Camp, we had the opportunity to work with the UNRWA camp-improvement program to create an open space—about seventy square meters—in a crowded neighborhood. When we approached the community, one of the main needs that became apparent—especially for the women in the camp—was for a space where their kids could play. Well of course, as urban planners and architects, this was immediately interpreted as a need for a plaza. So, we came back and told them that we wanted to design a plaza together with them.

It turned out that they were extremely anxious and worried about the mere idea of a plaza. Their first question was, If in the beginning of this camp, we decided not to build a roof in order to not jeopardize our right of return, what does it mean now to build a plaza? They asked themselves and us, Is this really the last stage of settlement? Does it mean we are finally accepting living here permanently? Furthermore, another, even more important concern arose: What does it mean to think of ourselves as a collectivity and not as individual refugees? Refugees have been looked at from the beginning as relief subjects. They are not considered a community. Their subjectivity is not considered political. Rather than a collectivity, they are taken to be a *collection* of individual relief subjects who simply need to

---

2 Alessandro Petti, Sandi Hilal, and Eyal Weizman, *Architecture after Revolution* (Berlin: Sternberg Press, 2013).

be sheltered and given aid. In that sense, to propose a collectivity was really very worrying for them.

These concerns are explained by Abu Rabih and Abu Rami, both considered among the founders of Fawaar Refugee Camp. Having already spent sixty years in exile, they are among those who witnessed the tents of the camp being replaced by masonry homes. Now they are living to see its inhabitants begin to consider the spaces between homes as well. Abu Rami remembers how difficult the decision to build concrete walls instead of maintaining the tents was. Would this move enable the world to forget that what the refugees really wanted was to return home to their villages, not to settle permanently in the camps? Now that they are not only building homes but also beginning to shape common spaces, is this another concession—another way of accepting the permanency of the camp and giving up the dream of return? Would the plaza be merely a wretched attempt to mitigate conditions of total subjugation? Is the plaza a physical indication that the refugees have abandoned their strategy of convincing the world of their misery by means of their architectural misery? Could it be that they are initiating a new strategy of capitalizing on their strengths as refugees rather than their weaknesses as victims?

Abu Rami's father had been among the main opponents of building more durable homes. No doubt he remembers his father telling him, "Son of mine, if you ever begin to enjoy your life in the camp, you will forget the land you came from." Would his father have even agreed to be part of the discussion taking place today? Is it historically acceptable to think about the public space of a temporary camp?[3]

Some of the camp inhabitants argued for the plaza as a representation of the power of its collectivity—one that would make the process of demanding political rights even stronger. Why fear it! Rather than erasing our political demands, they said, the plaza could be the place where we gather to claim our rights.

Once the debate was settled in favor of going through with the idea of a plaza, the next issue raised was that the community wanted the plaza to be a "closed" structure. Again, we were being confronted with an unusual challenge for urban planners and

---

3   Sandi Hilal, "A Plaza in a Camp: A Play in Four Acts," in *Architecture is All Over*, ed. Esther Choi and Marrikka Trotter (Barcelona: ACTAR, 2015).

architects: We had to ask ourselves what it would mean to create a closed plaza. We were faced with an instruction that the plaza—by definition an open space—must be closed. When we asked, What do you mean by a closed plaza? they explained very clearly that what they were aiming for was a place where people would not find themselves by chance. Anybody's presence in the plaza would always be an intentional act; they would actually have to decide, under their own responsibility, to enter. What they wanted was a walled plaza with four doors; so that, if you are merely passing by, you could go around it. You would need always to make a conscious decision whether to enter.

As Abu Ata later explained:

> You know, many people would prefer to hold their wedding ceremonies nearby their homes, for logistical reasons like food distribution. This is why, as a community, we are beginning to think about how to create similar plazas in other parts of the camp. The enclosure of the plaza was a very important step, I think, and absolutely essential. Imagine if the kids were to play soccer and kick the ball through one of the neighbor's windows. These kinds of accidents used to happen all the time, but now we don't have to worry about this issue anymore. The walls create a special and protected space, because a person who is simply passing through the neighborhood would never find himself in the plaza by chance. (Triumphantly) But now, with the new plaza's design, whoever is passing in the street can pass without interruption, and whoever wants to enter the plaza does so at their own risk, which means that the person has to accept the possibility that he might get hit by a soccer ball, which means in turn that if he gets hit by the ball, he will just laugh and be happy to be part of the game. For me, this is what makes this plaza a special one.[4]

That was the practical explanation, but we had wanted to understand more about why there was a need for people to be fully conscious of entering or not entering

---

4 Ibid.

the plaza. The neighbors of the plaza explained to us that in their situation of having no municipality or governing body, having no notion of public space, there can be no one responsible for taking care of, and maintaining, the plaza. Therefore, it is essential that those who decide to enter the plaza know that they will be responsible for whatever may happen to them in that space.

As we began the design of the plaza every one of the neighbors took part in deciding how high the surrounding walls would be, where the doors should be, what the plaza would look like. Once we finished the design and looked at it together with the community, we were surprised to find that in the end we had built the roofless home. We had accomplished in that space exactly what, since the 1950s, had been the idea of how to build a roofless camp. We had made a roofless plaza. It's not a private space and it's not a public space, it's both. So could we call this *Al-mashaa*? *Al-mashaa'* has been for us a way to think about how and where collectivity could take place. Now, we saw how it can be helpful in thinking about ways to approach architecture differently, to include a way of life beyond the two categories of public and private.

The refugee camp has always been perceived at the margin or periphery of the city. It has always been understood from the perspective of the city. Now, our invitation to you is to understand the city from the perspective of the camp. How the camp could become the representation of the common. To look at the world from the point of view of the refugee, the displaced person—not always from the point of view of the Western citizen. It is important for us to put the refugee at the center: to understand an architecture of the common, to understand *Al-mashaa'*. That is, to place the camp and the refugee, not the privileged figure of the citizen, in the center of our thinking.

EDITOR'S NOTE

This is an edited transcript of the thought experiment Sandi Hilal delivered to SUPPOSIUM 2014 via video hookup.

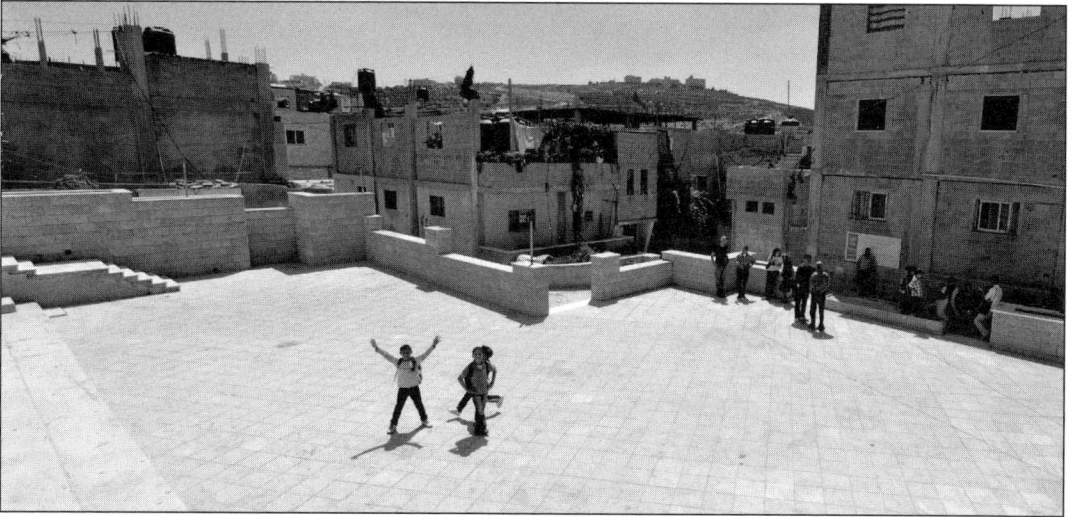

ADAM PENDLETON

Suppose to choose. To suppose is to choose.

His very words are action words . . .

Field notes from a sociolinguist:

Maaan, all performers are on stage at once—DJ Hi-Tek, Talib Kweli, Common, Biz Markie, De La Soul, Pharoahe Monch—and they just kickin' it in a fun-loving communal-type hip-hop atmosphere! Common and Biz are exchanging lines from his classic hit . . . the DJ from De La starts cuttin' up the music and before you know it, Common is center-stage freestylin'. The DJ switches the pace of the music, forcing Common to switch up the pace of his freestyle-improvisational rap, and the crowd's lovin' it! "Oooooooohhhhh!" . . . Hi-Tek and Maseo are circling each other on stage giving a series of hi-fives timed to the beat, smilin' and laughin' all along, as the crowd laughs on with them. Common, seizing the energy of the moment, says, "This is hip-hop music, y'all!" Then he shouts, "It ain't nuthin like hip-hop music!" and holds the microphone out to the crowd. "It ain't nuthin like hip-hop music!" they roar back, and the hall is transformed into an old-school house-party frenzy. . . . Gotta love this hip-hop music.

Reflections from a sociolinguist:

What is striking about this description is that there are multiple levels of call and multiple levels of response, occurring simultaneously and synergistically, to create something even beyond "total expression." This is a *multilayered totalizing expression* that completes the cipher (the process of constantly making things whole). We witness a call and response on the oral/aural, physical (body), and spiritual/metaphysical level. My final note ("Gotta love this hip-hop music") captures a moment of realization that

10 • SUPPOSE TO CHOOSE. TO SUPPOSE IS TO CHOOSE.

meaning resides in what I've just witnessed—in the creation of a continuum beyond audience and performer. We hear varied calls made by the DJ and responded to by a freestylin' MC; by the two MCs exchanging lines and by their impromptu leading of the audience in celebration of hip-hop; by the physical reaction of performers to each other and the audience (who were also slappin' hands with the performers); and by the spirited and spiritual response created during the climax of the performance. Like Common say, "Find heaven in this music and God / Find heaven in this music and God / Find heaven in this music and God."

I have been trying to find language for the recent deaths of Trayvon Martin, Jordan Davis

Language that occupies

That stands ground

We must . . .

take the mechanized hardware of the language of war apart by locating alternate evidence in multiple media, by questioning the pseudo-objectivity of its delusional conclusions, by unpacking its embedded metaphors and narrative frames, by thinking otherwise . . .

We must suppose

We must suppose to choose

Marching in New York, after the Martin verdict some chose to sing Ella's Song:

We who believe in freedom cannot rest
We who believe in freedom cannot rest until it comes

Until the killing of Black men, Black mothers' sons
Is as important as the killing of White men, White mothers' sons

We who believe in freedom cannot rest
We who believe in freedom cannot rest until it comes

We must choose to suppose

We must choose

Our language

I'd like to locate the/a continual present of a Black English

A language that:

. . . [requires] that you not only have a repertoire of vocabulary or syntactical devices/constructions, but you come prepared to do something in an attempt to meet the person on a level that both uses the language, mocks the language, and recreates the language.[1]

Some rules:

Eliminate *do* as in:

What do you think? What do you want? S. E.

What you think? What you want? B. E.

---

1 John Wideman, "Frame and Dialect: The Evolution of the Black Voice in American Literature," *American Poetry Review* 5.5 (1976): 34.

In general, if you wish to say something really positive, try to formulate the idea using emphatic negative structure.

He's fabulous. S. E.

He bad. B. E.

Use double or triple negatives for dramatic emphasis.

Tina Turner sings out of this world. S. E.

Ain nobody sing like Tina. B. E.

Never use the -ed suffix to indicate the past tense of a verb.

She closed the door. S. E.

She close the door. Or, she have close the door. B. E.

PLAY FIRST MINUTE AND TWENTY SECONDS OF "ELLA'S SONG" THEN FADE OUT

We who believe in freedom cannot rest
We who believe in freedom cannot rest until it comes

We who believe in freedom cannot rest
We who believe in freedom cannot rest until it comes

Until the killing of Black men, Black mothers' sons
Is as important as the killing of White men, White mothers' sons

We who believe in freedom cannot rest
We who believe in freedom cannot rest until it comes

. . . that which touches me most is that I had a chance . . .

His very words are action words

His very words are blues

What blues do you want to see?

What blues do you choose?

Macho man

Tell it to my heart

Tell it to my heart

A linguistic buffalo?

I came upon this recently . . . while writing this text . . .

Amiri Baraka writing to poet Edward Dorn in 1961:

"If my letter re your poem sounded crusadery and contentious I'm sorry. But I have gone deep, and gotten caught with images of the world, that exists, or that will be here after we go. I have not the exquisite objectivity of circumstance. The calm precise mind of Luxury. . . . I can't sleep. And I do not believe in all this relative shit. There is a right and a wrong. A good and a bad. And it's up to me, you, all of the so called minds, to find out. It is only knowledge of things that will bring this 'moral earnestness.'"

Thank you.

FRED MOTEN

S'posin' / Al-Mashà / A Mashup

S'posin' I should fall in love with you
Do you think that you could love me too?
S'posin' I should hold you and caress you
Would it impress you or, distress you?
S'posin' I should say "For you I yearn"
Would ya think I'm speaking out of turn?
And s'posin' I declare it,
would you take my love and share it?
I'm not s'posin', I'm in love with you.

Suppose we don't take place. Our thing would be sub-positional and we'd have to keep falling in love with that. We'd have to assume the apposition. Let it turn. Let's turn. Let's turn it out. Let's go out of turn and speak out from there. Suppose we derange. Suppose Diotima is Sassy. Suppose the intensity of the erotic relationship between Socrates and Razaf were given its due by those who claim to be concerned with virtue? Our pursuit is a rich braid of indirections. This plaited movement in stillness, where theme, variation and restatement of theme turn out to have been coterminous, is where difficulty and pleasure meet, in their essence, as practice, established as a strain and striation of questioning. If I were really courageous I'd be pure DJ: they tell us all we need to know by curving, that track they keep laying down, trane as garland, in open secret chambers, in the city of erotic brotherhood, for miles and miles and miles. But then there's what we need to know in order to get to that going through and getting past and running around, like riding the blinds of Hibbler's Tiresian croon. Socrates and Razaf are out of the way, across as well as along with Waller and Aristophanes, Pausanias and Tatum, Sinatra and Agathon, Alcibiades and Armstrong. What we talk about when we talk about love when you take my love and share it is the social situation of philosophy, which is given in generic impurity as a preoccupation with shift, a valorization of shiftlessness's disavowal of valuation. The social situation of philosophy is slavery. Find the fugitive in the text, the *metoikos* buried in the house, way on the outskirts of town, in the seam, apposed to meaning, and prefer her constant escape. Prefer the sub-positional flights of black and blue Garveyites, their non-spatial, atemporal arkestra. Suppose we constantly prepare that preferential option. Suppose we practice our practice. Suppose we study how to listen. Suppose we revolve. Suppose we make a circle of revolt in our repose, on our left shoulder, reclining as we eat, softly cutting one another as we serve one another in the absence of every other imposition except the general necessity, when the symposium explodes, antagonizes, unsettles into the general practicum. Suppose we strike that pose. Suppose we don't take place. S'pose I'm not sposin'. You know how it goes.

EDITOR'S NOTE

At the supposium, Fred Moten played Miles Davis's 5'17" version of *S'posin'* from his computer hooked into the room's speaker system before reading the above text. He did this without comment.

1. Performance Notes - a) Melody as played by Miles Davis

b) Optional introduction

2. Scales For Soloing (for chords with alterations)

3. Sample Piano Voicings (for chords with alterations)

4. Sample Bass Line

PETER KRAPP

Fall Guys: On Thought Experiments and Simulation

What if thought experiments were not only a way to articulate the pivotal but often obscured connections between fiction and simulation, between philosophy and science, between storytelling and critical argument, but also a way to reconcile the supposedly hard-science culture of computer simulation and the so-called artistic and humanistic tradition of posing critical questions? What if these two cultures in fact were one and the same, derived from the same stories and insights?

Another way to formulate that guiding supposition is to ask whether computers in fact do or do not give rise to a culture of the thought experiment that transcends and actualizes the status of the merely theoretical, fictional, imaginary. One of the most elaborate examples might be the recently rediscovered Rainer Werner Fassbinder film *World on a Wire* (1973), a low-budget yet highly inventive adaptation of the dystopian American novel *Simulacron-3* (1964) by Daniel Galouye about a corporation manufacturing a supercomputer that generates and supports a virtual world that is robust enough that the artificial intelligence entities in it believe themselves to be real. The film's setting in the Institute for Cybernetics and Futurology is portrayed as a labyrinth of reflections, steeped in art-historical allusions but entirely in the service of artificial life and simulated reality. Similar territory is pursued by Greg Egan's influential novel *Permutation City* (1994). Is consciousness merely information processed in certain ways, regardless of what machine or organ is used to perform that task? Or is this invalidated by reminding ourselves that a hurricane model does not make anything wet, a fusion plant simulator does not produce energy, a metabolic model does not consume actual nutrients—so a model of the human brain does not amount to giving rise to actual thought? What if cellular automata could, given enough time and processing power, evolve into a structure complex enough to permit flight from this planet and its constraints into a realm that is unlimited by everything that holds humanity down? What if every thought experiment, even as it pushes at the material constraints of our existence on earth, was by the same token partly practicing that step off-world, out of place, out of time?

Suppose you could overcome gravity and the grave? What if global warming, infectious diseases, overpopulation, and other urgent questions confronting humanity today could be addressed at the planetary level? This kind of thought experiment may seem like the province of science fiction (what if there was another planet that could sustain human life?)—but in this age of the rapid emergence of many dire emergencies, that supposition has become the pivot of our engagement with planetary problems. Our default mode of troubleshooting environmental, pedagogical, political, or aesthetic crises had been ad hoc, partial, local—but increasingly now, our problems are of a planetary scale, and require attention to possible solutions at a larger scale. A global response would require a model at a much larger scale—what if a large-scale solution to large-scale problems could be modeled, tested, improved, and deployed? What if all the various emergency responses demanding full attention were to be connected, on a scale that integrated them into a global geometry of attention, or a planetary model? What if one modeled that kind of whole-earth response?

Computers of course are much faster than human brains at chaining together complex branching cascades of what-if, what-if, what-if. So even if some may wonder whether computing is not also part of the problem, increasingly we assume that computing must be part of the solution, too. But let us slow down and look back on a longer history of simulation and thought experiments. There are numerous well-known examples both in science and in philosophy of thought experiments—whether we think of Maxwell's demon, Schrödinger's cat, the Turing test, or Searle's Chinese room. Outlining the trajectory of a brief history of the thought experiment, we may find that the gesture is somewhere between falling and throwing (yourself). In the history of science, serious thought experiments date back to the day Thales of Miletus (in Asia Minor or what is now the West Coast of Turkey), speculating about the stars above, fell into a well. Considered by Aristotle one of the Seven Sages of Greece, and by Bertrand Russell the first philosopher, Thales wanted to explain natural phenomena without reference to mythology. However, this pre-Socratic stargazer is said to have been observed falling into the well by a maid who laughed at his distracted tumble. So at the anecdotal origin, we also have to deal with a lack of recognition for the significant potential of the thought experiment. Moreover, it could also be said that what the anecdote highlights, by way of a dangerous absence, is the middle ground between transcendent gaze and empirical pragmatics. At any rate, Thales's rejection of mythology and insistence on testing hypotheses based on general principles establishes itself firmly at the core of the scientific process, of rational thinking.

Albert Einstein improved on the experimental setup when he observed a Berlin roofer tumbling down. Just like Thales, had the roofer not survived *and* been observed, our intellectual history would be so much the poorer, since he shares with the bystander Einstein the fact that during free fall he felt no gravity. This insight was gained without risk to Einstein's life and limb. When the need for complex calculations—such as ballistic trajectories and the fluid dynamics of weather and of explosions—challenges traditional methods, that significantly spurs the development of computing towards the end of World War II, and thought experiments start to be conducted more regularly "in silico." Yet this practice could build upon a long tradition in political consulting, military history, and in games. From antiquity to the eighteenth century, people knew chess, for instance, as a model of pre-gunpowder combat. The nineteenth century saw the Prussian *Kriegsspiel* adopted by other military commands as a way to prepare officers for informed decisions. And by the turn of the twentieth century, feedback from the front was regularly infused into training before experience grows stale.

Simulation is of course particularly useful in closed mechanical systems; one example is the airplane. Charlie Chaplin's half-brother Sydney (who had briefly formed the first privately owned domestic American airline, based in Santa Monica, California—it lasted less than a year) was a pioneer in offering flying lessons—but in fact he just flew his affluent clients around, and scared most of them away; he got out of the business after pilot licensing and air traffic regulations commenced. Not only were Syd's methods evidently not the best pedagogy, it was just as obvious that it would be costly to train people on the real thing—they can get hurt, expensive planes can be destroyed, so it is better to train pilots on simulators. In a quick distinction owed to the work of Claus Pias, one might say that action games today still mostly depend on the setup of a flight simulator providing instant feedback on twitchy controls, in the rhetorical order of the metaphor: this rolling log, this bucking bronco is a plane. This trajectory of throwing yourself into the sky in order not to fall continues from the wooden Link Simulator to the current generation of Microsoft Flight Simulator games. Mastering its controls in a first-person perspective affords the users a speed or other rush, transgressive thrills that please the Id. In the mode of role-play, the critical element is not so much time and speedy reaction as it is the making of decisions, in the rhetorical order of metonymy: you go this way or that way, you are dwarf or elf, you have long hair or short, as you perform the constitutive tasks of the Ego in a second-person perspective. And the third-person perspective of strategy games affords oversight, laying down rules like the Superego and seeing how they play out—tax rates, religious prohibitions, traffic laws, surveying the tabletop or board or floor game in the rhetorical mode of synecdoche, whereby a tank or a plane stands for armies, a tree stands for the forests cut down to make room for pasture in South America, and the critical element is neither a series of individual performative substitutions nor reaction speed but the coordination of large-scale systems.

For the most complex systems, such as epidemiology or economics, simulation can still be a good introduction to dynamic system behaviors, a way to explore options and test the validity of assumptions. When Alice falls down the rabbit hole, grabbing a jar of marmalade on the way down, the thought experiment is still a pre-global one: what if you fell right through the center of the planet? Would you accelerate and pop out the other side? Where would that be? When Lewis Carroll wrote in the 1860s, people could still suppose the Earth is hollow, and indeed hollow Earth theories remained popular until explorers fought their way to the North and South Poles. It was not until a century later that Buckminster Fuller seized the nascent planetary consciousness and suggested that we are all hurtling through outer space, that we are falling through nothingness on Spaceship Earth. His planning games, meticulously arranged on large maps that could cover the floor of a gym or conference hall, soon gave rise to computer-based planning exercises that shifted the metaphor further: Operating System Earth—how would you run the planet? It took a minimal observer's distance from the Earth to arrive at this new planetary consciousness—not by coincidence did the Apollo shot of the "blue marble" become the omnipresent logo of the green movement, the most trafficked photo in the history of mankind.

Today, there are a number of institutions researching simulation and its uses for government, military, and business: the Technical Support Working Group, the Modeling Virtual Environments and Simulation program at the Naval Postgraduate School, the Air Force Agency for Modeling and Simulation, the Navy Modeling and

Simulation Office, the National Simulation Center. But before we dismiss them as part of the military-industrial complex that has little to do with our cultural lives, let us remember that artists including Leonardo, Michelangelo, Dürer, and Galilei drew and built models of fortresses and of weapons. Closer to our time, it was famously the Tech Model Railroad Club whose elaborate play set and communication system gave rise to the MIT hacker scene. Of course, even when computer simulations use fundamental theory to generate models, they must beware of any confirmation bias and strive to use simulations as tests of the underlying theory.

Given that more and more of our most pressing problems are global in scope and cause, an interesting extension of the trajectory of simulation is the Living Earth Simulator or Large Knowledge Collider proposed by Swiss sociologist Dirk Helbing. To predict infectious disease outbreaks, combat climate change, or foresee financial crises, Helbing wants to connect the knowledge of domain experts across all scientific fields with a large-scale real-time data mining capacity. His grant proposal to the European Union asked for funding of a billion euros. Resembling to some critics the Seldon Plan, which you might recall is named after Isaac Asimov's fictional character Hari Seldon of the Foundation series, the Large Knowledge Collider would simulate all systems that are critical to managing our planet.

To wrap up, the task of strategy games had the flow of data as its driver, optimizing command and control, but their trade-off is that they are slow. Simulations sought to offer safe training driven by feedback principles, optimizing survival, but the trade-off is that those systems need to abstract and omit variables. Equation-based modeling took that logic into the computer age, driven by complex calculations, optimizing the predictive value of the model, but the trade-off is that the computer models become a black box. Agent-based modeling sought to improve on this setup in a distributed model, driven by artificial intelligence, optimizing individual behavior, but the trade-off is that they are very decentralized. The Living Earth Simulator or Large Knowledge Collider takes global modeling as its task, driven by data mining technology to optimize collective behavior. Of course, the trade-off of such a totalizing model is that . . .

Oh, I'm out of time.

ANNE CARSON

Suppositional Preface

WHAT *preface* IF

Suppose I am to deliver a lecture on a work of art (*Seated Figure With Red Angle* by Betty Goodwin); and suppose the grammar of the language in which I have to give my lecture is one composed exclusively of conditional sentences—there are no other kinds of sentences—how to proceed? On the hypothesis that what I most want to do in front of a work of art is stay silent, or at least hesitate, and therefore I have nothing final to say about this painting despite my obligation to lecture on it, it seems best to proceed by making my lecture entirely out of if-clauses. A conditional sentence, as you know, has two parts: the if-clause (or protasis) and the then-clause (or apodosis). If I express only the protasis of a condition, no finality is arrived at and I can keep the hesitation in. That is, taking as an example the sentence, *If I loved you then I would marry you*, notice how different is the mood obtained by abbreviating to simply, *If I loved you*. How thick and interesting the silence that falls after *you*.

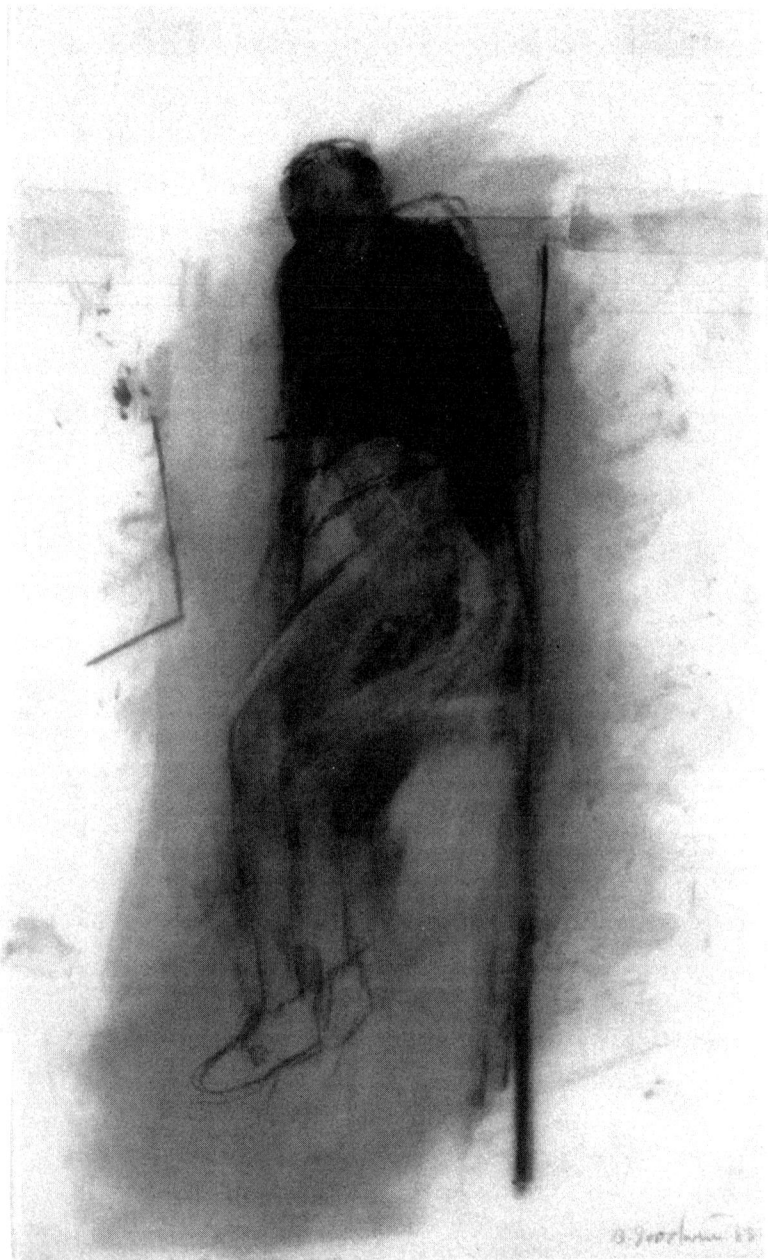

BETTY GOODWIN, *SEATED FIGURE WITH RED ANGLE*, 1988. MIXED MEDIA, CA.
14 ⁹/₁₆ × 9 ¹/₁₆". IMAGE COURTESY OF *ARTFORUM* MAGAZINE.

SEATED FIGURE WITH RED ANGLE (1988)
BY BETTY GOODWIN

If body is always deep but deepest at its surface.

If conditionals are of two kinds factual and contrafactual.

If you're pushing, pushing and then it begins to pull you.

If police in that city burnt off people's hands with a blowtorch.

If quite darkly colored or reddish (bodies) swim there.

If afterwards she would sit the way a very old person sits, with no pants on, confused.

If you reach in, if you burrow, if you risk wiping in.

If a point that has been fed over years becomes a little bit alive.

If the seated figure started out with an idea of interrogation.

If there was a quality of very strong electrical light.

If you had the idea of interrogation.

If interrogation is a desire to get information which is not given or not given freely.

If buried all but traceless in the dark in its energy sitting, drifting within your own is another body.

If at first it sounded like rain.

If your defense is perfect after all it was the trees that walked away.

If objects are not solid.

If objects are much too solid.

If there are no faces, if faces are not what you interrogate.

If red makes you think of chance or what chance operates with.

If the feet cross in a way that sucks itself under, sucks analogies (Christ) under.

If as Artaud says anyone who does not smell cooked bomb and condensed vertigo is not worthy of being alive.

If you choose what to undo, if you know how you make that choice.

If you lead her to water.

If you bring her a gift say one of Pascal's thoughts.

If you bring "infinite fractions of solitude" (Nabokov).

If you bring a bit of Artaud like "all writing is shit all writers are pigs."

If conditionals are of two kinds possible and impossible.

If she slides off, if you do.

If red is the color of cliché.

If red is the best color.

If red is the color of art pain.

If Artaud is a cliché.

If artists tell you art is *before thought*.

If you want to know things like where that leg is exactly.

If the horses were exhausted.

If she begged, if she came to the table, if the sequence doesn't matter.

If it begins, a trickle, this thin slow falling of the mind.

If you want to know why the sliding affects your nerves.

If you want to know why you cannot reach your own beautiful ideas.

If you reach instead the edge of the thinkable, which leaks.

If you stop the leaks with conditionals.

If conditionals are of two kinds real and unreal.

If nothing sticks.

If she waits alongside her.

If Miroslav warned us that experimental animals should not be too intelligent.

If to care for her is night.

If an enigma came into the room.

If all the other enigmata fought to get out.

If outside of here the light has gone from the tops of the trees that rise over a brick wall opposite.

If conditionals are of two kinds now it is night and all cats are black.

If how many were killed by David exceeds how many were killed by Saul by tens of thousands.

If they don't feel pain the way we do.

If you drove here with toys in the backseat.

If you wrote a word on the floor of the cell in waterdrops and videotaped it drying.

If Vitruvius says no temple can be coherently constructed unless it is put together exactly as a human body is.

If red is the color of italics.

If italics are a lure of thought.

If Freud says the relation between a gaze and what one wishes to see involves allure.

If you cannot remember what word you wrote.

If art is the servant of allure.

If Vitruvius does not talk about taking temples apart but we may assume the same canon applies.

If there is no master of allure.

If conditionals are of two kinds allure and awake.

If no matter how you balance on the one you cannot see the other, cannot tap the sleep spine, cannot read what that word was.

If "contrafactual" applied to conditionals means the protasis is false.

If (for example) "had you not destroyed the barometer it would have forewarned us" implies that we are now standing in a storm of rain.

If as a matter of fact it is a clear night I would say almost relentlessly clear.

If conditional comes between condiment and condolence.

If you do not want to remember what word it was.

If your life bewilders you (*sly life*).

If the rain lashes your face like manes of all the horses of this century.

If conditionals are of two kinds graven and *where is a place I can write this*.

II
MANIFESTOS, CONVERSATIONS

Black Dada

1.

it's a matter of fact

2.

it's a matter of fact

a full moon hanging in a low sky irradiates the day with a milky glow

4.

it's a matter of fact

going in a taxi from the train station

a full moon hanging in a low sky irradiates the day with a milky glow

i was with nielsen living and painting in a north beach flat

8.

it's a matter of fact

a full moon hanging in a low sky irradiates the day with a milky glow

i was with nielsen living and painting in a north beach flat

going in a taxi from the train station

and then somebody kicks off the lid

sigh and then breathe

these buildings don't uncover a single truth, so which truth do you want to tell?

the grant is 800 euros

16.

it's a matter of fact

a full moon hanging in a low sky irradiates the day with a milky glow

the grant is 800 euros

it's theological; it's a revelation

going in a taxi from the train station

and then somebody kicks off the lid

need i cite charles van doren

on a stool in a greasy spoon

human beings were born to live in a relationship of interdependence with nature

the performance must be done on location

regular communication by email with a commitment to responding within a
reasonable time frame

the performer must not be credited

a revolving door

she was a unit in a bum space; she was a damaged child

so did i love

architecture is bound to situation

32.

it's a matter of fact

a full moon hanging in a low sky irradiates the day with a milky glow

now i am older and wiser

going in a taxi from the train station

she was a unit in a bum space; she was a damaged child

so did i love

regular communication by email with a commitment to responding within a reasonable time frame

sigh and then breathe

the performer must not be credited

and then somebody kicks off the lid

it's theological; it's a revelation steel bell drops

the grant is 800 euros

on a stool in a greasy spoon

need i cite charles van doren

i want the grey-blue grain of western summer

i want the cardboard box of wool sweaters on top of the bookcase to indicate home

i want a very beautiful woman

a common doubt expressed about the "practice-based" researcher is whether they are equipped for "competent reading"

the performance must be done on location

these buildings don't uncover a single truth, so which truth do you want to tell?

the desire for coffee

the formal beauty of a back porch

remember the wedding?

dada is our intensity

i want a very beautiful man

when a work of architecture successfully fuses a building and situation, a third condition emerges

i think what black arts did was inspire a whole lot of black people to write

monuments are embarrassing to dutch culture

revolving door

song of the garbage collectors beneath the bedroom window

seeds of the fig

64.

it's a matter of fact

a full moon hanging in a low sky irradiates the day with a milky glow going in a taxi from the train station

now i am older and wiser

she was a unit in a bum space; she was a damaged child

the formal beauty of a back porch

and then somebody kicks off the lid

i need the grey-blue grain of western summer

i need the cardboard box of wool sweaters on top of the bookcase to indicate home

i need a very beautiful woman

steel bell drops

when a work of architecture successfully fuses a building and situation, a third
condition emerges

what black arts did was inspire a whole lot of black people to write

Black Dada, black dada

this is dada's balcony, i assure you

from there you can hear all the military marches, and come down cleaving the air
like a seraph landing in a public bath(s) to piss and understand the parable

i had a nice dick, average length and all

i wanted ron to look at it, want it

dada is our intensity; it erects inconsequential bayonets and the sumatral head of german babies

i need a very beautiful man

it's theological; it's a revelation

the grant is 800 euros

need i cite charles van doren on a stool in a greasy spoon

how are we to define this poem?

what makes you think that's what this is for?

what do you want for christmas?

does it mean that if the universe is infinite, then in some other world a man sits in a kitchen, possibly in a farmhouse, the sky lightening, and nobody else up and about as he writes down these words?

i want the perfume back in the bottle

i need a prick in my mouth

i need an explanation

what did you think when they converted the funeral home into a savings and loan?

revolving door

dry blood

song of the garbage collectors beneath the bedroom window

seeds of the fig

white dada remains within the framework of european weakness

the essence of architecture is an organic link between concept and form

pieces cannot be subtracted or added without upsetting fundamental properties

we want coherence

she was a unit in a bum space; she was a damaged child, sitting in her rocker by the window

i want western movies

i need monday morning, a prick in my mouth and coffee

a cigarette and coffee for two

primal soup

pineapple slices

Black Dada is a way to talk about the future while talking about the past; it is our present moment

a common doubt expressed about the "practice-based" researcher is whether they are equipped for "competent reading"

yellowing gauze curtains

remember the wedding?

the raised highway through the flood plain

regular communication by email with a commitment to responding within a reasonable time frame

so did i love this

the performer must not be credited

the performance must be done on location

feet, do your stuff

sigh and then breathe

i want a young man with long eyelashes

white wings of a magpie

red shingle roof

i'm unable to find the right straw hat

how will i know when i make a mistake?

presentness

soap

we ate them

128.

it's a matter of fact

she was a unit in a bum space; she was a damaged child

a full moon hanging in a low sky irradiating the day with a milky glow

the formal beauty of a back porch

but now i am older and wiser Black Dada

The Black Dada must ...

The Black Dada must use irrational language.

The Black Dada must exploit the logic of identity.

The Black Dada's manifesto is both form and life.

can you feel it?

does it hurt?

is this too soft?

do you like it?

do you like this?

is this how you like it?

is it alright?

is he here?

is he breathing?

is it him?

is it hard?

is it cold?

does it weigh much?

is it heavy?

do you have to carry it far?

what about dinner?

The Black Dada is neither madness, nor wisdom, nor irony.

song of the garbage collectors beneath the bedroom window

look at me, dear bourgeois

dada is a new tendency in art

art used to be a game of nuts in may, children would go gathering words that
had a final ring, then they would exude, shout out the verse, and dress it up in
dolls' bootees …

one can tell this from the fact that until now nobody knew anything about it, and tomorrow everyone in zurich will be talking about it

Black Dada: we are not naive

Black Dada: we are successive

Black Dada: we are not exclusive

Black Dada: we abhor simpletons and are perfectly capable of an intelligent discussion!

DA DA DA DA DA DA DA TK TK TK TK

thus saith the lord

i need ron to look at it, want it

i need a beautiful woman

i need the cardboard box of wool sweaters on top of the bookcase to indicate home

i need western movies

i need the grey-blue grain of western summer

Sol LeWitt exhibited his Variations of Incomplete Open Cubes in the early 1970s.

Which is to say LeWitt's Paragraphs on Conceptual Art (1967) and Sentences on Conceptual Art (1969) had already been written.

In 1969 a young June Jordan dedicated her poem "Who Look at Me" to her son Christopher:

We come from otherwhere

In part we grew by looking back at you

BLACK DADA.

Malcolm X arrived in Harlem in the early 1950s.

In 1952 John Cage composed his famous silent work 4' 33".

At the Meredith March in June 1966, a year before LeWitt wrote Paragraphs on Conceptual Art, Stokely Carmichael arguably laid the foundation for the Black Power movement.

In a talk given at the University of Massachusetts, Amherst on the 6th of November 2006, Kathleen Cleaver asked:

The 1960s, is that something that still makes you stand up and notice? Do you still notice the 1960s?

Hugo Ball read his Dada Manifesto at the first public Dada soirée in Zurich's Waag Hall on July 14th, 1916:

Dada psychology, dada Germany cum indigestion … dada literature, dada bourgeoisie, and yourselves, honored poets, who are always writing with words but never writing the word itself, who are always writing about the actual point. Dada world war without end, dada revolution without beginning, dada your friends and also-poets …

Dadaism in the wake of the First World War.

Public gatherings.

Demonstrations.

Art of protest.

BLACK DADA.

Did our conceptual artists join hands with our freedom fighters?

Did they demonstrate in Birmingham?

Did they cover their faces when the hoses were turned on them?

History is in fact an incomplete cube shirking linearity.

BLA K DA   . B   DA. BLACK D D .

a common doubt expressed about the "practice-based" researcher is whether they are equipped for "competent reading"

feet, do your stuff

sigh and then breathe

i want the perfume back in the bottle

i want a prick in my mouth

i want a young man with long eyelashes

regular communication by email with a commitment to responding within a reasonable time frame

so did i love (this)

the performer must not be credited

the performance must be done on location

props and sets must not be brought in

the sound must never be produced apart from the images or vice versa

any cameras for documentation must be handheld

special lighting is not acceptable

optical tricks and "effects" are forbidden

the performance must not contain superficial action, declarations or jokes

temporal and geographical alienation are forbidden

genre performances are not acceptable

the format must be set: 30 minutes, 20 minutes, 1 hour

white wings of a magpie

red shingle roof

steel bell drops

wave glory

soap

presentness

human beings were born to live in a relationship of interdependence with nature

the desire for coffee

how will i know when i make a mistake?

the grant is 800 euros

does it mean that if the universe is infinite, then in some other world a man sits in a kitchen, possibly in a farmhouse, the sky lightening, and nobody else up as he sits and writes down these words?

if the function of writing is to express the world

i need an explanation

i'm unable to find the right straw hat

Black Dada is a way to talk about the future while talking about the past

History is an endless variation, a machine upon which we can project ourselves and our ideas

that is to say it is our present moment

The history of conceptual art as (is) an intimately constructed narrative deserving of an aggressive deconstructive interpretation.

An iconic structure that embraces linearly passive readings of its ideological principals and the moment of its "coming into being."

the raised highway through the flood plain

pineapple slices

we want coherence

we want a revolving door

song of the garbage collectors beneath the bedroom window

seeds of the fig

white dada remains within the framework of european weakness

i need monday morning and a prick in my mouth

a cigarette and coffee for two

what does it cost?

do you speak english?

do you hear a ringing sound?

are you high yet?

is he the father?

are you a student at the radio school?

what is it that attracts you to bisexual women?

do you know which insect you most resemble?

did you know i have a nice dick, average length?

did you know his cum is the eighth color of the rainbow?

do you know what it tastes like?

but now, look at me, we don't agree with them, for art isn't serious, i assure you, and if we reveal the crime so as to show that we are learned denunciators, it's to please you, dear audience, i assure you, and i adore

but now i was older and wiser

black dada your history of art

we ate them

In Conversation

Words are essential in Adam Pendleton's art. The artist's engagement with experimental prose and poetry over the past ten years, along with his cross-referencing of visual and social histories, has made space for new types of language within conceptual art. Pendleton's largest U.S. museum show to date, *Adam Pendleton: Becoming Imperceptible*, opened at Contemporary Arts Center New Orleans in April, before traveling to the Museum of Contemporary Art Denver, where it is on view through September 25.[1]

ALLIE BISWAS (RAIL): You made an instrumental move in getting your career off the ground by taking your art to galleries and making them look at it. There's a story that your work was included in a show in New York at Gallery Onetwentyeight, the director of which assisted Sol LeWitt, and that's how LeWitt saw your work.

ADAM PENDLETON: Yes, that's true. Those earlier works (almost) always incorporated language, for one. Otherwise, there was a system to how the thing was composed. So I was convinced that, even though visually they looked like abstract painting, they were very much conceptual. That was actually the most gratifying thing, of course, when LeWitt came into the gallery and commented on my work. Whatever view on this paternalistic language and its historical accuracy, he's been called the father of conceptual art, so when he said, "Oh, I like this!" I was this young kid who was totally sure of this already and could turn around

---

1 *Adam Pendleton: Becoming Imperceptible* was on view at the Contemporary Arts Center New Orleans from April 1, 2016 to June 16, 2016 and at the Museum of Contemporary Art Denver from July 15, 2016 to September 25, 2016. This interview was originally published in *The Brooklyn Rail* on September 1, 2016.

and say to anyone who would listen, "See, it is conceptual!" [*Laughter.*] But who knew why he was drawn to the piece. I never had the opportunity to talk with him about it, but we did trade at the time.

Some of the earlier works I appreciate more than others, like any artist. But for me, it was all happening in public. So I sometimes think that I basically went to art school in public. I did my first solo show in New York at Yvon Lambert in 2005, and I did a project at Wallspace in 2004 just before that. I was twenty.

BISWAS: It sounds a bit absurd, doesn't it?
PENDLETON: Now it does. [*Laughter.*]

BISWAS: What was happening to your work and your process during this time?
PENDLETON: The work changed, and—I guess because of my age—I was very open to that. I think a lot of what art students are trying to do is related to trying to find something—the thing that they feel "works." You look around, and it does seem like artists who have had any kind of trajectory have been able to maintain a kind of logical progression of their work. So I think a lot of people are trying to find that first thing that works for them. But actually, the thing that works is learning how to manage the chaos of making art. That's what really works.

BISWAS: Your performance from 2007 [*The Revival*] caught the attention of a lot of people. Would you agree that this work took your career in a different direction?
PENDLETON: That was when my own thinking about my work changed dramatically, yes. You have all of these ideas, and then you realize that what you make can't be a half-step toward those ideas. You actually have to manifest it. So I had this idea of taking a Southern-style religious revival, and turning it on its head, and then fusing it with experimental language. It was really that simple. I think it was the first time I had the idea to deconstruct, reconfigure, and reimagine an existing form and ask: what else could this be? What happens if you remove the religious aspect, but you leave the gospel music, the musical component? What happens if you take out the religious language that's related to queer activism or contemporary poetics? It was about creating a capacious space, breaking down one form and creating something else.

BISWAS: Was *The Revival* the first time that you had made a performance?

PENDLETON: On that scale, for sure, but I had been collaging texts and making performances before that.

BISWAS: When did language start to be laid into your photographic painting works?

PENDLETON: Well, language was always an important part of my life. I used to write poetry—don't all teenagers write poetry? [*Laughter.*] It's funny that, while things have changed a lot, they haven't changed much at all, and I think a lot of this was just the environment that I grew up in. My mom had Adrienne Rich's books in the house and June Jordan and Audre Lorde, so I was reading their work when I was very young. My dad was a musician—not professionally, but he played music when he was at home. In many ways I think that we are a product of our environment, although I am not inclined toward reading people's biographies to make sense of who they are and what they do. My brother and my sister were in the same house and they're not artists. But of course you see these things going on, and they piqued my interest. But there was also a political drive from a very early age. I always thought that art was something that could effect change, and I think that in a strange way that was the real drive. What could I do that would actually change things around me, or change how we imagine the world and our built environment? Art was this thing that could shift attention.

BISWAS: Maybe now is a good time to talk about Black Dada, which could be read as connecting language to a political drive.

PENDLETON: The paintings that I showed in my first solo show in New York were text paintings, and they appropriated the writing of people like Toni Morrison, Rich, Jordan, and Lorde. They basically attempted to represent the cadence of someone speaking the words that were visually present. They were two-color silkscreens, and I think quite special in a way. Linguistically, they referenced one poetic tradition, but in terms of layout and so on they had a concrete poetry aspect, though less austere somehow than that might sound. They were quite erotic and loving. Later I became introduced to writers like Joan Retallack, Ron Silliman, Leslie Scalapino, and Charles Bernstein.

BISWAS: What impact did those writers have on you?

PENDLETON: Reading their work caused a big shift in my own work. It wasn't a visual thing. It had more to do with theoretical positions around language, going from one school of thought—I guess you could call it a lyrical school, which the poets I was reading had a very political foundation with regards to content— to a very different school, which was more aligned with how conceptual artists thought about language: language as material. So there was this productive overlap between language, conceptual art, lyrical poetry, and activism—whether formal or content-based or both. I didn't feel it necessary so much to take sides. I wasn't a poet as such, and think I took from the different genres or schools what felt useful at that time. *The Revival* was the first time those ideas were presented publicly and cohesively, and it just happened to be a performance. Black Dada, in one sense, represents the things that I started to do with language in a visual space following *The Revival.*

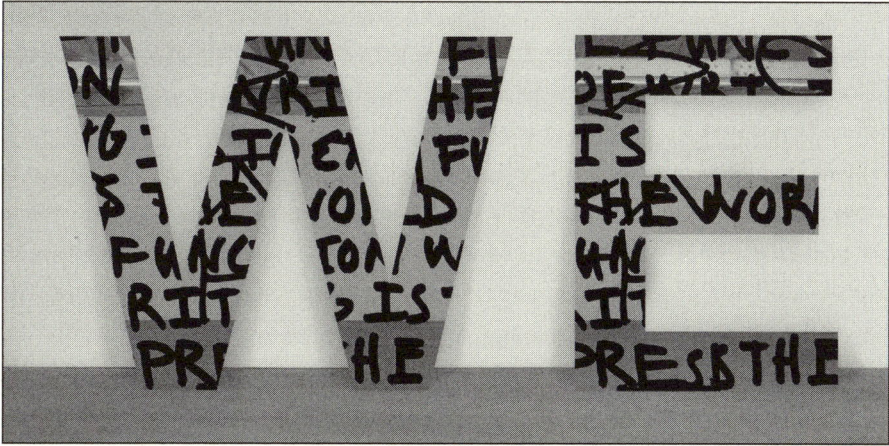

ADAM PENDLETON, *WE (WE ARE NOT SUCCESSIVE)*, 2015.
SILKSCREEN INK ON MIRROR POLISHED STAINLESS STEEL.
46 13/16 X 61 1/2 X 5/8 INCHES (W) 46 13/16 X 35 5/8 X
5/8 INCHES (E). COURTESY THE ARTIST.

BISWAS: So this political drive was the foundation for how you were approaching everything that you were making. But what was the actual intention?

PENDLETON: Black Dada is an idea. When pressed, I often say it's a way to talk about the future while talking about the past. It surfaced in a conversational space, when I was just talking to friends. I had Amiri Baraka's book *The Dead Lecturer*, which contains the poem "Black Dada Nihilismus." I found the language striking: "Black" as a kind of open-ended signifier, anti-representational rather than representational. And then "Dada"—sort of nonsense. A sound, but also referencing a moment in art. So this language became a productive means to think about how the art object can function, and does function, in the world. What can art do? I think all artists should be asking themselves this question. Not "what is it?" It's whatever you want it to be, but what can it do? What do you, as an artist, want it to do? Black Dada also became a way to create a conversation and to insert my work into conversations about appropriation that I was observing at that particular time, in about 2008. I don't know if you remember how everyone was talking about appropriation around that time, as though it was something new, and it, of course, wasn't. So it was a way to shift perspectives, but it also, again, created space for myself as an artist. I still reside there as an artist, but I keep pushing it and trying to change the shape of it, and of the space(s) it creates.

BISWAS: And you put together a Black Dada book. How did that develop?

PENDLETON: I created a reader, yes. That began as a conversation with Jenny Schlenzka, who is a curator at MoMA PS1, about this idea of Black Dada in relationship to institutions, and how it could change institutional dynamics. The reader is essentially organized into three different sections: "Foundations"—so, foundational ideas to Black Dada, which are represented in text by thinkers from W.E.B. Du Bois to Gilles Deleuze to Stokely Carmichael—and then it shifts into "Language," which includes a range of writers whose works I've been drawn to such as Harryette Mullen, Retallack, Jordan, and others. The third section is "Artists' Positions," which collects texts by or about artists whom I relate to Black Dada, including Ad Reinhardt, Joan Jonas, and Stan Douglas, who is represented by his screenplay for *Inconsolable Memories*. It's going to come out next year for a show I'm doing in Berlin. The original version was spiral-bound, really an old-school reader. The version that is being published will include the content of the original reader along with essays by curators and critics who have engaged deeply with Black Dada including Adrienne Edwards, Laura Hoptman, Tom McDonough, and Susan Thompson.

BISWAS: I'm currently working on an anthology of black art, which compiles texts that were written by and about artists in the 1960s and '70s. At present there isn't any publication like it that people can refer to. You wonder, why does this sort of book not already exist?

PENDLETON: It's interesting that you say that, because around that time, in 2007, I started to think that a lot of gestures that I had made were actually retroactive. I felt that I was creating something that should have existed ten, twenty, forty years ago. It was like I was inserting things into the art-historical canon. For example, with the Black Dada paintings—which relate formally to modernist painting and the monochrome—I was infusing that space with very different language, quite literally, and also sort of messing it up. Messing it up slightly, but a lot at the same time, so it's also a contradiction, this duality, how a little bit is *a lot*. So, again, maybe these paintings were made in 1914. It's illogical. What did LeWitt say: "Illogical judgments lead to new experiences."

BISWAS: Tell me about your residency at MoMA.

PENDLETON: The initial aspect of it is over, yet the broader project continues. It was an incredible opportunity to interact with the collection, but also with the institution, in a more intimate fashion. It was really just the institution saying, "Let's see what happens."

BISWAS: So what did happen? And how does the context of a residency affect your way of working?

PENDLETON: The one problem I have with residencies is that I don't really like working in places outside of my own spaces. I like to be around my books, my things. I can't really pack up the studio and go to Beirut. So I thought about my work in relationship to the institution in an antagonistic way. I also thought about what kind of discursive or formal gesture I could make that could disrupt the ebb and flow of how this very large entity functions. I began a conversation with Joan Retallack—who is an essayist and poet, and who used to teach at Bard College—saying, "What if we did something at this place, at the Museum of Modern Art? What could we do?" At the time I was reading a short text that was published for Documenta 13 by Michael Hardt titled *The Procedures of Love*, and so I was initially going to do something around that text, whether that be a public conversation with Hardt, or something else. In the text, and this is a real summary, he talks about the political potential of embracing difference. In essence, potential resides in the differences between us, not in the similarities. I started talking to Joan about this and she went back to this idea of love and eros, and to Plato, to the Symposium. She conceived this event called SUPPOSIUM 2014 and the basic premise was that she invited different people—myself, along with poet Anne Carson, Sandi Hilal of Decolonizing Architecture, film theorist Peter Krapp, and literary theorist/poet Fred Moten—to give talks that began with the word "suppose." So "Suppose…" That was the conceptual conceit, or the point of departure: *suppose*.

BISWAS: How was the event executed?

PENDLETON: We delivered the talks in MoMA's Founders Room to about 100 participants. Each person was asked to take notes during the talks of phrases or words that captured their attention, and then these notecards were collected and redistributed, and we created a kind of group text from these fragments. As I say this to you now I realize that in a strange way SUPPOSIUM 2014 did somehow articulate what Hardt was talking about. Joan described it as a procedural thought experiment. For me, it became this question about how to have productive dialogues. How can we have productive public conversations and exchanges? How do we repurpose this idea of "I'm talking and you listen?" How does that become more about call and response? That was also a key aspect of *The Revival*: call and response and community through difference, something that has often been a key to black music as well.

BISWAS: During SUPPOSIUM 2014 you talked about Black Lives Matter. You had previously used the slogan in your installation in the Belgian Pavilion at the Venice Biennale in 2015, but prior to this you had shown paintings in London, earlier on in the same year, that incorporated these words.

PENDLETON: Yes, my show in London was the first time that I exhibited work using that language. But the subject matter came up during SUPPOSIUM 2014, because that was shortly after George Zimmerman was found not guilty for murdering Trayvon Martin. I was asking the question, "What language stands its ground?" "Stand Your Ground" was the law that created the legal gray area where Zimmerman got off. He was "standing his ground." I thought: we need language that stands its ground.

BISWAS: So you were reacting in real time, as it were. It's not as though two years went by after these incidents took place, and then you decided to respond through your work.

PENDLETON: I couldn't help but respond to the absurdity of the situation. It was the absurdity of it all coupled with the ongoing task I've set for myself of figuring out what Black Dada is. It is a kind of "black space" one could say. It is also a social space—it creates a social space. I think it gave me the room to respond to Black Lives Matter, even just on the level of the language. They are both very clear short statements.

BISWAS: And you were looking at these two statements in relation to each other.

PENDLETON: Beyond anything else, I wanted to look at them in relation to each other—first as an artist, but then as a citizen. And in that context, as a citizen, there was another set of concerns. Jenny and I joined the protest in New York after the Zimmerman verdict. They had to close down Times Square for a short period of time. People were singing "Ella's Song" by Sweet Honey in the Rock: "We who believe in freedom cannot rest until it comes." Just thinking about the role of voice in general, and how Occupy Wall Street was a collective voice, but there was no individual voice that rose above all others. During the protests against the Zimmerman verdict, I was looking for a voice. There were different utterances, but you could tell that no one really knew how to speak, which fascinated me for many different reasons. Was that an evolution? Something new and important? Or was it somehow a weakness? So it was almost as though, after that, I was asking, "Does 'Black Lives Matter' function? Does this language function? What can it *do*, what does it do?" and I brought those questions along with others into the visual and conceptual space of my work.

BISWAS: Is Black Dada shorthand for "This is Adam?"

PENDLETON: No. It's a kind of refusal.

BISWAS: Regardless, people understand that you're not coming to it in this very straightforward way—

PENDLETON: —In 2008 I was invited by curator Krist Gruijthuijsen to be a part of a show he curated within Manifesta 7 called *it's a matter of fact* and I ended up writing a Black Dada manifesto. Basically it was a system for collecting sentences. So the first line of my text is the title of his exhibition *it's a matter of fact*, and then it collects. So it goes from one, two, four, eight, sixteen, thirty-two, sixty-four, et cetera, accumulating a repeating series of sentences that are also attracting new language to them as it evolves. In effect it is the theoretical underpinning of the Black Dada project, it deliberately aligns aesthetic/political distinctions, creating a chronology-based affinity between conceptual art and political actions in the '60s, for example, which had this conceptual and performative intelligence. What always fascinated me was that shortly after I wrote that, I read it publicly in a few places. But then the graphic designer/artist Will Holder also started reading the text around the world in quite different places, and I love this idea of Holder as my doppelgänger or something. You know, going around as the ambassador of Black Dada. It's so simple—the "Black" and the "Dada." But you're right, there is nothing straightforward about it.

BISWAS: By taking the hashtag Black Lives Matter and inserting it into the work, and being in a position where you can present it widely, do you think that you are one of the only artists to have really gone public with it? Do you think this has given you a kind of "credibility" in the minds of certain other people, in the sense that they are presented with an artist who feels very strongly about this current moment in time and he has acted upon it? Given the expression's widespread usage, obviously through social media in particular, its popularity could perhaps even be viewed as "fashionable." That sounds inappropriate, but I think you'll understand what I'm getting at.

PENDLETON: You're the second person to use the word "fashionable." The thing is that there are stakes involved in everything that we do. This is paraphrasing the words of Rachel Blau DuPlessis: my intention as an artist is not to use the modes and methods of protest in the sense of saying, "This is wrong" and "That is right." It is, however, to draw attention to things at times, in different ways through different registers. So I wanted to bring it out of the space of actual fashion, where things are short. Occupy Wall Street, in a strange way, is like the past already, even though it's not, and even though it impacts everyone's life. The same thing with Black Lives Matter—you have it in the media and everyone's talking about it. In 2013 it came about and now, in the mainstream media, it's like, "Oh would they stop carrying on" or, "Okay, we get it" or, "They're interrupting Bernie Sanders now? Don't they know he's on *their* side?" Again, this language *has* not and *will* not leave the space of my work. It was about bringing a different kind of rhetoric and attention to the language, to the moment, to the movement.

BISWAS: It was about extending the temporary space that it exists in, and creating a legacy.

PENDLETON: Let's bring Black Lives Matter into the temporality that art objects and discourse can often afford. I showed these paintings in a show at the Museum of Contemporary Art Denver in 2015 and the local art critic came around and said, "Oh, yes, these are nice paintings but this is so yesterday. Six months ago maybe this would have meant something, but it just seems so old." There is the case in point— "this is so old" —when actually these are things that as a country we have been grappling with for hundreds of years. It is neither new nor old.

BISWAS: For those who appreciate the importance of not forgetting about this moment in history, you have made sure that it doesn't get forgotten about.

PENDLETON: —Which goes back to that question about how things function retroactively.

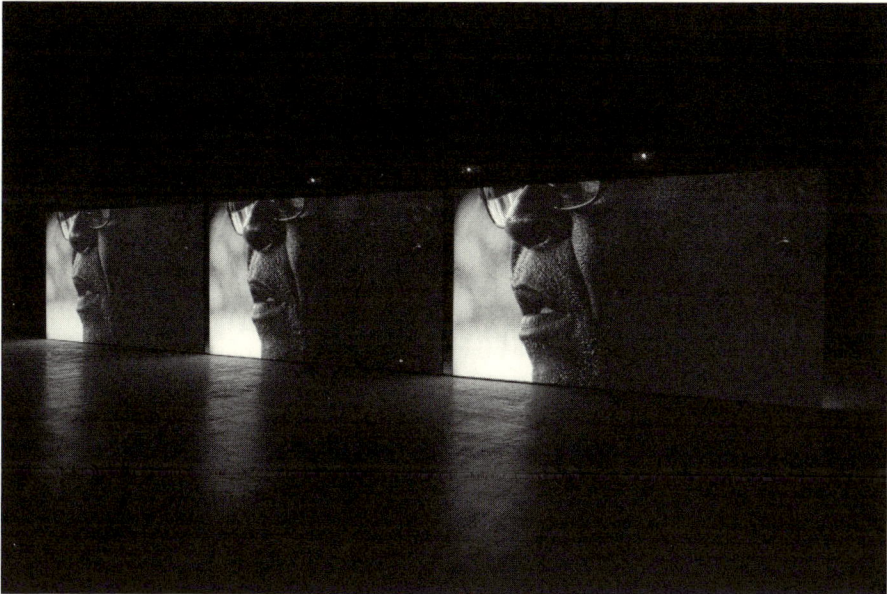

ADAM PENDLETON. *MY EDUCATION: A PORTRAIT OF DAVID HILLIARD*, 2014. THREE-CHANNEL BLACK-AND-WHITE VIDEO, 9 MINUTES 19 SECONDS. COURTESY THE ARTIST.

BISWAS: Let's talk about your show, *Becoming Imperceptible*, which was presented at the Contemporary Arts Center New Orleans this year, and has now traveled to the Museum of Contemporary Art Denver.

PENDLETON: I wonder what people will make of it when they see the exhibition because the work is very slow moving. It's open but also hermetic and a lot of the decisions and steps I make are very slow and deliberate. And not necessarily in a way that I think would be readily apparent to anyone else. So I am curious.

BISWAS: The show is curated by Andrea Andersson. What conversations were you having with her?

PENDLETON: Andrea has a Ph.D. in comparative literature, and she has a background in contemporary poetry. So that's actually where the conversation started. Then we moved to how I think about ideas of representation, of politics and abstraction—how these two things relate— which is how my body of work has evolved: from language, to language and image, to a more abstracted or abstract space. So in exhibition, we really thought about the operation of each floor.

BISWAS: It's a substantial exhibition—you cover three floors.

PENDLETON: Yes. We thought critically about the operation of each floor The first floor is visually similar to the installation I conceived for the Belgian Pavilion in 2015. It is maximalist, a kind of system of displaying a complete overview of the work. There's a distinct visual rhythm. It's a collage in space.

BISWAS: What happens on the next floor?

PENDLETON: On the second floor things begin to empty out, and you begin to see that very much in the work itself. I use one piece to create another piece to create another piece. It becomes a part as a whole or a whole as a part. But again this idea of how to represent something comes up, modes and mechanisms of representation. What is a fragment? So you have a portrait of Satomi Matsuzaki, the lead singer of Deerhoof, whom I filmed for a 2009 three-channel video called *Band*. She is taken out of the space of that original, which documents Deerhoof in a recording studio working on a new song, and it now exists as a six-second loop where all you see her do is turn her head. It's just on repeat, an index of a larger work. Then the same thing happens with Baraka's poem "Black Dada Nihilimus." I represent it through a wall painting that lists almost all of the proper nouns from his text in the order that they appear. It's a kind of visual note taking.

Then you have the "System of Display" works, also on the first floor, which began by using many images, but now use very few images and again look at the question of what bears the burden of representation. Is it the language or the image? How do they function together? There are also ceramic floor pieces that I made via the influence of "clairvoyant poet" Hannah Weiner. Then, as you move up to the third floor, this idea of portraiture that began with the loop of Satomi carries over, but this time it's a video portrait of David Hilliard, who was Chief of Staff of the Black Panther Party. This portrait is related to another I made of Lorraine O'Grady and both are partially influenced by Gertrude Stein's textual self-portraits.

BISWAS: What are the final works that the viewer encounters?

PENDLETON: Three large, five-foot by ten-foot silkscreens on mirror-polished stainless steel that are based on a photograph of water taken by Josef Albers. They're hung in a raw, corridor-like space along one wall. In the end, they look like abstract columns that distort the viewer's image of her- or himself. The show encompasses various historical references, from the Bauhaus to Malcolm X to the Black Panthers to Godard. The objects carry these histories and ask them to coexist in a way—to ask, what is their potential?

BISWAS: How do you make the works? I have read a lot about the role of photocopying in your practice.

PENDLETON: A lot of the things I do are very matter of fact. Let's say for the Black Dada paintings, I use an image of LeWitt's incomplete open cubes: Xeroxing it, cropping the Xerox, scanning it, enlarging it, and then laying this text over top of it. I take an object and do something to it, and then do something else to it. I would say everything is some sort of collage and has always been. This is true even in the earlier works that didn't necessarily look like a collage, because what I was doing was taking someone else's language and then I was sort of inserting myself on top of it—inserting my own rhythm and my own mode of presentation.

BISWAS: What is appropriation for you? What is that doing within the work?

PENDLETON: To borrow or steal? It's a complicated question. I think that's why I'm very slow, because I have to create the space where a kind of transition can occur—where it can go from being an image of an incomplete open cube to a mark or a line. That's a conversation that you have with the material, slowly, over time. Now, because I've been using these images, these materials for so long, I no longer even think of my use as an act of appropriation. I think about it in a more discursive sense of just being in conversation with, or rubbing against, something. I said once that we are appropriated as human beings, that's what we are. I mean, how can anything be anything other than appropriation—which is why the term is so loaded and also so over-determined.

FRP (Feminist Responsibility Project)

YELLOW JACKET, 2013

DALMATIANS, 2013

MONEY, 2013

EARS, 2011

GLOVES, 2011

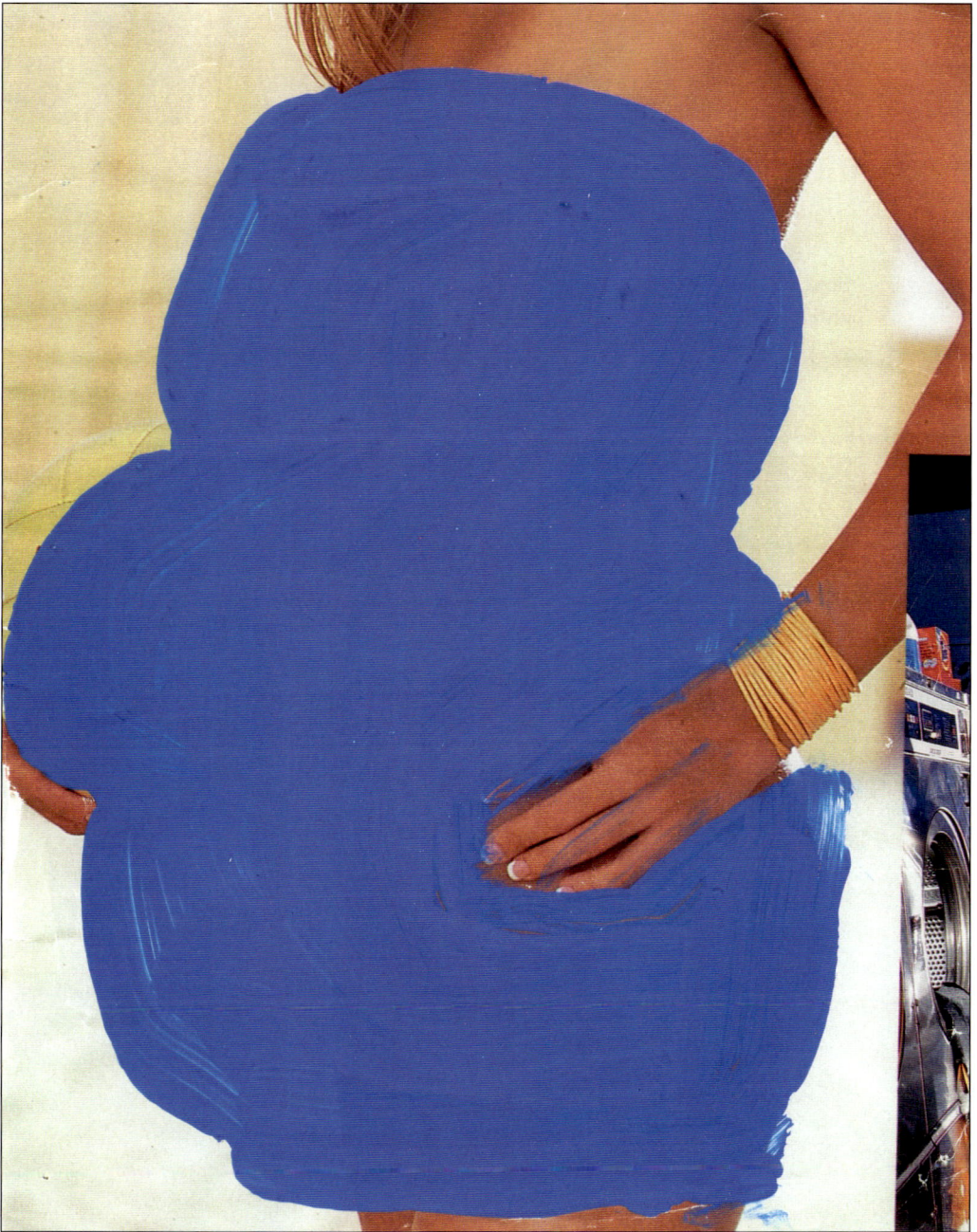

BLUE DRESS, 2005

Yellow Jacket, 2013
Ink on magazine page
7 ⅜ × 6 in.

Dalmatians, 2013
Ink on magazine page
10 ⅝ × 7 ⅞ in.

Money, 2013
Ink on magazine page
10 ½ × 7 ⅞ in.

Ears, 2011
Ink on magazine page
10 ¾ × 6 ¾ in.

Gloves, 2011
Ink on magazine page
10 ¹¹⁄₁₆ × 6 ⅞ in.

Blue Dress, 2005
Paint on magazine page
6 ⅝ × 5 ¼ in.

INGRID SCHAFFNER

Beverly Semmes's FRP: An Induction

What is the Feminist Responsibility Project? And why is Beverly Semmes in charge of it? By the time Semmes emerged as an artist, the first wave of Feminism had already subsided, transformed from a political form of activism to a cultural form of reference. Semmes is part of a generation who made their mark during the early 1990s with a Feminist take on Minimalist art of the 1960s. Think of the monumental, monochromatic, mostly metal, always hard monoliths of such artists as Donald Judd, Carl Andre, and Richard Serra. Now apply fabric, fashion, the body, craft, appetite, desire, excess, because that's exactly what Semmes—along with such peers as Janine Antoni, Polly Apfelbaum, Kiki Smith, Jessica Stockholder—seemed to be making sculpture with, for, and about.

For instance Semmes's *Red Dress*, 1992, now in the collection of the Hirshhorn Museum and Sculpture Garden. As big as the wall, and attached to it by a hanger, this gargantuan velvet gown cascades to the floor, where it pools and pushes us out of the way like a coming tide, a red tide. Get it? The metaphors and imagery of Beverly Semmes's art typically flow in this direction: from the female body and out into the landscape. Dresses are to be seen as vessels, as Semmes's pots made of out glass and clay demonstrate. Like cartoon images of "making a pot," these sculptural objects are gruntingly physical embodiments of the touch, the craft, the pleasure, and work that goes into building even the most elemental of forms. Whether it's pots or dresses, Semmes's works are environmental in sensibility and scale, billowing, icy, earthy, aqueous, or luminous, depending on material and color, which are always superabundant and sensational.

There is also a performance aspect to Semmes's work. The dress sculptures can appear as costumes, worn by gallery attendants as part of an exhibition, or by models in Semmes's photographs and videos. The latter are usually family members and friends. (Getting people you care about involved with your work is always important.)

Semmes too performs on occasion. She sometimes dons wig and sunglasses to deliver a talk, or, even, while working. As an artist-in-residence at Pilchuk Glass School, Semmes must have struck a glamorous note, hanging around the glory hole (as the fiery center of the foundry is called) in a patently '70s getup.

The seventies were, of course, also the heyday of Feminism, which brings us back around to the original question. The Feminist Responsibility Project—or, to use the artist's acronym, FRP—made its debut at Rowan University Art Gallery in the form of an installation with video, sculpture, photography, and two performers. The immediate impression was of a setup so highly stylized and strange that it must stand for something. But what? The floor was covered in a foamy sea of white chiffon fabric, in the midst of which two women in voluminous gowns sat on chairs, facing one another. One woman's gown was striped, the other's a kind of canine camouflage, all-over-dog print. As identified by their attire and other insignia, the women were characters, the "Super Puritan" and "Bitch." They were doing a picture puzzle, spread out on a table between them. Overhead hung a beautiful chandelier, handcrafted of clear molten crystal; it was lusciously globular.

There were pictures on the walls. A projection covering one (like Warholian wallpaper, a picture that moves) with a video of a woman's feet, kicking a potato over a frozen lake. The potato, painted pink, messes the ice and makes a dull thudding noise that filled the gallery space. On the other walls hung a series of pictures that come straight from the core of Beverly Semmes's Feminist Responsibility Project.

For more than a decade, Semmes has been diligently collecting and correcting images from what she refers to as "gentlemen's magazines." This is a ladylike (Semmes hails from the South with roots in Arkansas and Alabama) reference to her sources: vintage Hustler and Penthouse magazines, the pornography of which she has masked with strategic coats of paint. And if the five FRP works included at Rowan[1] were anything to judge by, this project is much less straightforward than it may sound.

---

1 Semmes has since had comprehensive exhibitions of her FRP work internationally as well as at Susan Inglett Gallery (Chelsea, NYC) in 2014. From the Susan Inglett press release: "The Feminist Responsibility Project (FRP) is a collection of images and objects produced by crude gestures and the application of ink and paint to defile pornography."

For one thing, despite Semmes's "corrections" it's completely obvious that we are being confronted with shots of classic American porn. Splayed, spread, sucking on things, the women are more masked than concealed by paint-jobs that only amplify their objectification. Now things get tricky and funny, too, since the female objects on view are now simultaneously crude consumer objects of male desire and highly crafted feminist works of art. Focus on the painted parts and you see these silhouettes, the scale and shapes of which look a lot like Semmes's sculptures: tactile, oversized, sensual, scatological, enveloping, grotesque, humorous, basic. If you grabbed any one of these painted forms and set it on the floor, you would see one of Semmes's pots or dresses. Masked in color, all of Semmes's forms specify the body as something elemental with a hole in the center.

The provocation of the hole lay at the center of the Rowan FRP installation. The female attendants sat inside an erogenous "O" of fabric on the floor. (And of course, in porno-parlance, women are just holes.) So what is the puzzle that the Bitch and the Super Puritan are piecing together? It's an FRP image that Semmes sent to a company in Germany that will turn any picture into a jigsaw puzzle. Speaking of puzzles, now seems like a good moment to introduce some of Beverly Semmes's own notes about her installation. The use of fabric and craft, she writes, are intended to reference first wave Feminist art practices with their infusion into the mainstream of women's work and decoration. The potato-kicking feet are flat-footed Freudian phallic symbols. Doing puzzles together is a favorite way of passing time with her mother.

Like any sacred ceremony or mystery play, Semmes's installations—with their fetish objects, icons, and acolytes—look just sanctimonious and serious enough as to appear a little ridiculous to those of us who stand outside them. Is this how Feminism looks today? Would only a bitch or a prig challenge the common wisdom that women have achieved equal opportunity as well as control over their own bodies? Has anyone been paying attention to Congress's gambit to slash support for Planned Parenthood? Or, on a lighter note, has anyone read Tina Fey? The most successful woman in comedy has written about her experiences coming up with the guys who dominate her profession. From an essay in the *New Yorker*, here is one of Fey's more pithy observations: "I have a suspicion—and hear me out, because this is a rough one—that the definition of 'crazy' in show business is a woman who keeps talking after no one wants to fuck her anymore." Caustic, funny, fearless, I love this quote: it's the Feminist Responsibility Project at work.

Taken as a whole, Beverly Semmes's FRP is a kind of camp. It disrupts the normal flow of pornography by strategically amplifying the awkward and obvious construction of the pose, the gaze, the exploitation, and the bodies that make it work. And it calls to order Feminism, along with social issues and political responsibilities that, in so-called Post-feminist culture, we may not care to embrace. Beverly Semmes's FRP shows us that Feminism retains the super-bitchy, pure-crazy power to prove that we are no way near finished with the project.

AUTHOR'S NOTE:
This essay was written just three years ago, before the vulgar objectification of women became part of public speech."

III

THOUGHT EXPERIMENTS, CONT'D

My Nobel
Prize-Winner

A few years ago,
I learned that a
scientist I had once
worked for had won
the Nobel Prize.
This was something
of a surprise.
When I first met
Marty, he was just
setting up his first
laboratory as a
junior professor.
He was a nice,
enthusiastic guy,
and obviously very
smart, but had none
of the off-putting
arrogance that
attaches itself to
certain scientists
when they are young.
I'd recently given up
the idea of becoming
a biologist in order
to write and was
making my living as
a technician, the
lowest position in
the lab hierarchy.

1

The New York Times

Three Chemists Win Nobel Prize

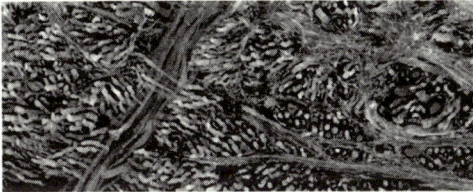

Brain cells of a laboratory mouse glowing with multicolor fluorescent proteins.

By KENNETH CHANG
Published: October 3, 2008

One Japanese and two American scientists have won this year's Nobel Prize in Chemistry for taking the ability of some jellyfish to glow and transforming it into a ubiquitous tool of molecular biology for watching the dance of living cells and the proteins within them.

Related

Three Physicists Share Nobel Prize (October 8, 2008)

The fluorescent proteins are now routinely used for observing the growth and fate of specific cells like nerve cells damaged during

☐ SIGN IN TO RECOMMEND
✉ E-MAIL
📱 SEND TO PHONE
🖨 PRINT
REPRINTS
SHARE

1 *New York Times*, October 8, 2008

EVELYN REILLY • 79

2

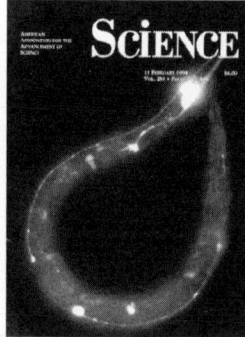

3

4

2 Flourescent jellyfish
3 *Science*, 263, 1994
4 Dr. Martin Chalfie

Now Dr. Martin Chalfie was being awarded the Nobel Prize in Chemistry for his use of a naturally-occurring protein found in certain jellyfish. It turns out that the gene for this protein, when spliced into the DNA of almost any animal, under certain conditions causes cells within the animal to fluoresce green in ultra-violet light. The prize wasn't, of course, given for Marty's ability to produce fluorescing animals per se, but for the fact that he had inserted this gene into a transparent worm about the size of a comma and studied how various other genes in its cells are turned off and on during the worm's development—one of the most fundamental questions of biology being how a ball of identical cells becomes a organism comprised of systems of complex differences. *Caenorhabditis elegans*, which means "horny-mouthed and elegant," is now a very famous worm.

Speaking of elegant, there is a photograph on the website

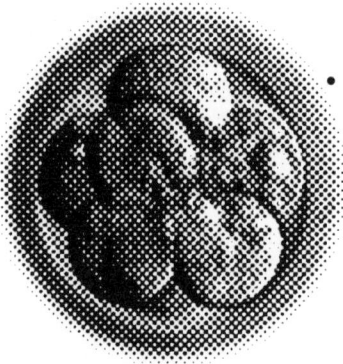

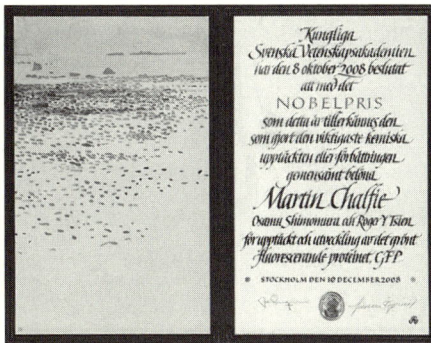

www.nobelprize.org of Marty wearing
a tuxedo and blowing a kiss to the
audience in Stockholm. I think it's
likely that the kiss was addressed
to his wife, Tulle Hazelrigg, also
a scientist. There is also a page
on the website where Marty's Nobel
lecture is posted. In the credits
at the end, he includes everyone
who has ever been part of his lab,
including all his lowly technicians.

Thus I treasure a rather bad
photograph taken in Marty's office
a few months later in which he is
showing me the very pretty hand-
lettered citation that all Nobel
laureates are given. This photograph
was taken during a reunion organized
by colleagues and former students
after his return from Stockholm. What
the photo doesn't convey is that at
the very same moment I was supposed
to be meeting the performance artist
Carolee Schneemann at the Bowery
Poetry Club for her appearance in
the Segue Reading Series, which I was
hosting that month. In fact, just a

5 Martin Chalfie and me, 2009

6 Nobel citation

7 Martin Chalfie,
   New York Times,
   October 8, 2008
8 Carolee Schneeman,
   artforum.com,
   March 5, 2007

Opposite
9 Leonard Nimoy as Spock
10 Emily Dickinson

few minutes before the picture was
taken, I had been down in the main
meeting room telling Marty that I had
to leave, when he said, "Do you want
to see my medal?" How could I say no?

So we spent some time together in
his office, which for me was a very
memorable experience, and then finally
were walking toward the elevator when
Marty began talking about his favorite
novel by one of the South American
magical realists. I was listening and
also thinking about Carolee, who had
called earlier sounding extremely
stressful because a heavy snowstorm
was on its way, but Marty was standing
between me and the elevator button
deep into recounting this incredibly
intricate plot and all I could think
was: a) I hate magical realism, b) I
am actually having a long conversation
with one of this year's Nobel Prize
winners, and c) What about Carolee?

I was literally caught between
my two muses: science and the
feminist avant-garde.

The Mask of Spock   I'd been thinking about the muse
recently, because I'd just read an
essay by Arnold Kemp titled "If Sambo
Were a UFO," which makes the case that
Spock, the Vulcan science officer
of the starship Enterprise, could
be read as a black character.[b] Kemp
argues that the ultra-logical Spock
displayed parallel characteristics
to the impeccably intelligent, but
emotionally-underdeveloped "black
science officers, inventors, and
technically-proficient operators
of advanced computer equipment"
that emerged on television just
as the achievements of the Civil
Rights Movement were manifesting
themselves. This made me ask—if
Spock can be read as black, can he
of the ambiguous smile and raised
eyebrow also be read as female?

Kemp's point was that in spite of
the overt multiculturalism of the
crew of the Enterprise—aka American
capitalism in full expansionist
exploratory enthusiasm—pretty
much all of the technical staff

were nonetheless deprived of
the fullness of personhood and
moral complexity of the white
male leaders. I would expand that
to say that all the technicians
were, in some ways, inferiors
of Spock, who, in spite of being
alien, was a "white male alien."

All these ambiguities are very
interesting and it would be
intriguing to trace the evolutionary
lineage of TV Spockism through
other geeks of the genre such as
Dee, the disciplined communications
officer of Battlestar Galactica (in
which, notably, a class of robot
"super-servants"—the Cylons—rise
up against their human creators)
as well as more recent examples.[c]
But what interested me more was
another aspect of the phenomenon,
that of self-selection, of what it
means to *choose* to don the mask of
Spock in its various guises as both
aesthetic and social strategy. To
what extent, for example, was Emily
Dickinson's "telling it slant"—which
included a lexicon of exoticism
and even a tactic of scientific
appropriation—a means of productive
indirection, of fruitful intellectual
play, and to what extent was it
protective coloration, a circuitous
strategy for success in a poetic
domain where female gender was
synonymous with marginalization?

As Susan Howe, the master of the
poetics of marginalia, has noted:

"Emily Dickinson took the scraps from the separate 'higher' female education many bright
women of her time were increasingly resenting, combined them with voracious and
'unladylike' outside reading…[and] built a new poetic form from her fractured sense of
being eternally on intellectual borders… Pulling pieces of geometry, geology, alchemy,
philosophy, politics, biography, biology, mythology and philology from *alien territory*…" [d]

Taking this method of operation as
a broad definition of something
that might be called Vulcan Feminist
Poetics, I wondered if aspects of
it were applicable to the working
procedures of some female poets today.

This precipitated a number of questions:

In what ways is such a strategy an embrace of the world, a
tool of investigation, even an exploration of gendered life?

In what ways is it a flight or reprieve from gender?

Is wearing the mask of Spock, a way of masking out issues of
class, race, sexual orientation?

Or is donning the drag of lab a means of claiming a clear
space, a place to hang free of the taboos and codifications
of ones particular "avant" moment?

Is it inevitable that every movement birthed in a spirit
of emancipation eventually coagulates into its own set of
forbiddens?

Is this why in advancing the garde, the Feminist Vulcanist
so often finds herself advancing her own guardedness?

Does "success in circuit" remain the operative term?

Is the Vulcanist's quest "to go where no man has gone
before"—the goal of masters of the universe?

Or is it a search for a home—the goal of exiles?

What if, unlike the crew of the Enterprise, we are no longer sailing into a capacious unknown, but instead, like that of the Galactica, are just trying to get from one devastated home to the next?

Is it possible that Vulcanism is not an evasion at all? Could it be that the Vulcanists, like the Cylons, are the ones redefining the struggle in the largest terms?

For example, whose galaxy is it?

Vulcan Poetics   What appeals to me about what I've come to think of as "Vulcan Poetics" —which includes, but goes beyond its feminist aspects—are the many arenas of investigation that radiate out from this kind of thinking.

Possible Vulcanist Investigations:

1. multiple language worlds
2. material being (aesthetics, erotics, ethics)
3. un-personism (the anonymous as the ultimate communal)
4. the technological sublime
5. our destiny as animals[c]

I find the first of these particularly intriguing, having come to realize that in my case, the muse doesn't look like either Marty or Carolee, but more often takes the form of what might be called "language sets"—vocabularies and syntaxes that constitute specialized worlds and their meaning systems.

Tangram Technology
Periodic Table of Thermoplastics

TANGRAM TECHNOLOGY — Consulting Engineers

Increasing performance →

Commodity | Engineering | Performance

Increasing crystallinity

Amorphous / Semicrystalline

Amorphous

Random molecular orientation in both molten and solid phases.

General Characteristics
Generally transparent,
Lower Tensile Strength and Tensile Modulus,
Low Creep Resistance,
High Dimensional Stability,
Low fatigue resistance,
Easy to bond using adhesives and solvents (high surface energy).

Semicrystalline

Random molecular orientation in molten phase, densely packed crystallites in solid phase.

General Characteristics
Sharp melting point,
Generally translucent or opaque,
Higher Tensile Strength and Tensile Modulus,
High Creep Resistance,
Low Dimensional Stability,
High fatigue resistance,
Difficult to bond using adhesives and solvents (low surface energy).

Amorphous row:

PS-HI (High Impact Polystyrene), PS-GP (General Purpose Polystyrene), ABS (Acrylonitrile Butadiene Styrene Copolymer), SAN (Styrene Acrylonitrile Copolymer), PMMA (Polymethyl methacrylate / Acrylic), PPO (Modified Polyphenylene Oxide), PC (Polycarbonate), PAR (Polyarylate), PSU (Polysulphone), PES (Polyethersulphone), PPSU (Polyphenylene-ethersulphone Block copolymer)

PVC-P (Plasticised Polyvinylchloride), SBS (Styrene-Butadiene-Styrene Copolymer), SMA (Styrene-Maleic Anhydride Copolymer), ASA (Acrylonitrile Styrene Acrylate Copolymer), SB (Styrene-Butadiene Copolymer), PEI (Polyetherimide), PAI (Polyamideimide), PI (Polyimide)

PVC-U (Unplasticised Polyvinylchloride), CA (Cellulose Acetate), CAB (Cellulose Acetate Butyrate), CAP (Cellulose Acetate Propionate), CP (Cellulose Propionate), PET-G (Glycol modified Polyethylene terephthalate), PVC-UX (Crosslinked Unplasticised PVC), PVC-C (Chlorinated PVC), PBI (Polybenzimidazole)

PVC-U (High-Impact Unplasticised PVC)

Semicrystalline row:

PE-LD (Low Density Polyethylene), PE-LLD (Linear Low Density Polyethylene), PE-MD (Medium Density Polyethylene), PMP (Polymethyl pentene), EVA (Ethylene vinyl acetate 12% VA), PARA (Polyaryl amide), PPA (Polyphthalamide Amorphous), PPA (Polyphthalamide), PEEK (Polyetheretherketone), PEK (Polyetherketone), PTFE (Polytetrafluoro-ethylene), PVDF (Polyvinylidene fluoride)

PE-C (Chlorinated Polyethylene), PE-VLD (Very Low Density Polyethylene), EMA (Ethylene methyl Acrylate), PE-X (Crosslinked Polyethylene), PE-UHMW (Ultra High Molecular Weight PE), PB (Polybutene Polybutylene), PA 6/3/T (Amorphous polyamide), PA 12 (Polyamide 12 / Nylon 12), LCP (Liquid Crystal Polymer Aromatic copolyester), PA 46 (Nylon 46), PCTFE (Poly-chlorotrifluoro-ethylene), ECTFE (Ethylene-chlorotrifluoro-ethylene)

PP (Polypropylene), PP (Polypropylene Homopolymer), PP (Polypropylene Copolymer), PBT (Polybutylene terephthalate), PA 66 (Nylon 66), PA 6 (Nylon 6), PA 11 (Polyamide 11 / Nylon 11), PA 12, EVOH (Ethylene vinyl Alcohol), PFA (Perfluoroalkoxy), PPS (Polyphenylene Sulphide), FEP (Fluorinated ethylene propylene), ETFE (Ethylene-tetrafluoro-ethylene)

PE-HD (High Density Polyethylene), PET (Crystalline polyethylene terephthalate), PA 6/10 (Polyamide 6/10 / Nylon 6/10), PA 6/12 (Polyamide 6/12 / Nylon 6/12), PA 6/12, POM (Polyoxymethylene / Acetal Copolymer), POM (Polyoxymethylene / Acetal Homopolymer)

KEY TO MAJOR POLYMER FAMILIES:

Styrenes | Polyvinyls | Cellulosics | Vinyls | Polyesters | Polymers | Polyamides | Polyacetals | Acrylics | Sulfones | Polysulphones | Fluoropolymers

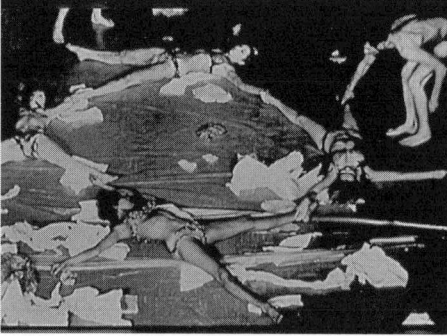

There was a time when I was
particularly enraptured by industrial
specification sheets, which led
to writing a book of poetry called
Styrofoam. It wasn't, however, just
these language sets, but also their
associated visual representations,
which, in terms of aesthetic impulse,
suggested possibilities not totally
disconnected from work I admired such
as Jackson Mac Low's "Light Poems" or
Heather Fuller's poems incorporating
veterinary emergency forms and Kristin
Prevallet's image-text works.

I also think of Vulcanism as a means
of engaging with "the world" in the
largest sense, because it entails
seeing language as deeply embedded in
materiality, not just in the sense
of being an artistic or plastic
medium, but as *an action of material
being*. In this way Vulcanism can
be seen as a continuation of the
feminist exploration of a revised
erotics of materiality, which was
advanced by many of the 1st wave of
2nd wave feminist artists, including

Previous Page

11 Periodic Table of
Thermoplastics

12 Carolee Schneeman,
Meat Joy, 1964

13 Carolee Schneeman,
Ask the Goddess,
performance 1993-97

14 **15**

Schneemann in works such as *Meat Joy* and *Ask the Goddess*, as well as in her "cooking" performances, a video of which she showed at Segue that day.

I've also been interested in the work of the artist Vija Celmins, particularly her paintings of things such as the surfaces of rocks, expanses of ocean waves, and images of galaxies. Like many visual artists, Celmins has a materialist way of thinking, but what particularly interested me was how expansive her view of "the material" could be. One could argue that all of her works are actually images of *material surfaces* — whether they are of the puff of smoke from a revolver, an expanse of lunar dust, or the surface texture of a historic photograph (the surface of a surface in that case).

14 Vija Celmins, *Ocean*, 2005

15 Vija Celmins, *Galaxy #4 (Coma Berenices)*, 1974

There was a time when I imagined writing an entire book absent the human presence—and I'm still very taken with this impossible and self-contradictory idea. It is impossible in the way that painting the "surface" of the cosmos is impossible, but I wanted to play with the idea of a poetry that was species independent or maybe at best species-neutral. This impulse came from a restlessness with the persistent retrograde anthrocentrism of poetry (another absurd and contradictory sequence of words, I realize), and an increasing discomfort with our notion of our "species position" and with the way current language supports that position. Maybe a better way to put it is that I had a desire to try to use this species-specific tool, language, in a project of repositioning the human subject within a new inter-species context.

In some ways I see this as an attempt to amend yet another messy inheritance of the Enlightenment—the positioning of art at the pinnacle of human achievement, in contrast to its pre-Enlightenment location somewhere between the human and transcendent. Not that I am advocating a return to the latter, but it does seem that another severe relocation is needed, this time involving a coming to terms with our "destiny as animals" and a radical rethinking of how we manage the Manichean nature of our ever-evolving tools—language being one of them—as both destroyers and emancipators.

As a poet, this desire has sometimes taken the form of trying to use language to enact a sense of geological or evolutionary time, or

Opposite
16 Ernst Haeckel's
  "Tree of Life," 1879

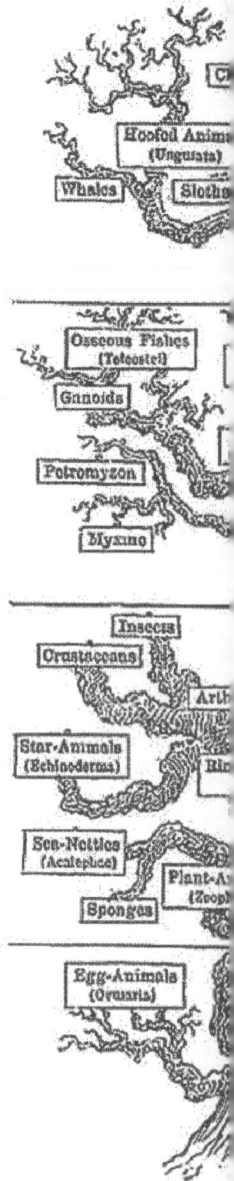

CE OF MAN.

Orang
Gibbon
Bats
Rodents
Beasts of Prey
-Apes
(eidea)
als
ammals
malia)
Hoofed Animals.

Mammals
(Mammalia)

Birds
(Aves)
Reptiles
Tortoises
Crocodiles
Lizards
Snakes
Tissues
als
Amphioxus

Vertebrates
(Vertebrata)

Ascidians
Salpæ
Animal
Sea-Squirts
(Tunicata)
Soft Animals
(Mollusca)
Soft Worms
(Scolecida)
Worms
inthes)
Worms
(Vermes)

Invertebrate Intestinal
Animals
(Metazon Evertebrata)

Infusoria
amoeba

Primitive Animals
(Protozoa)

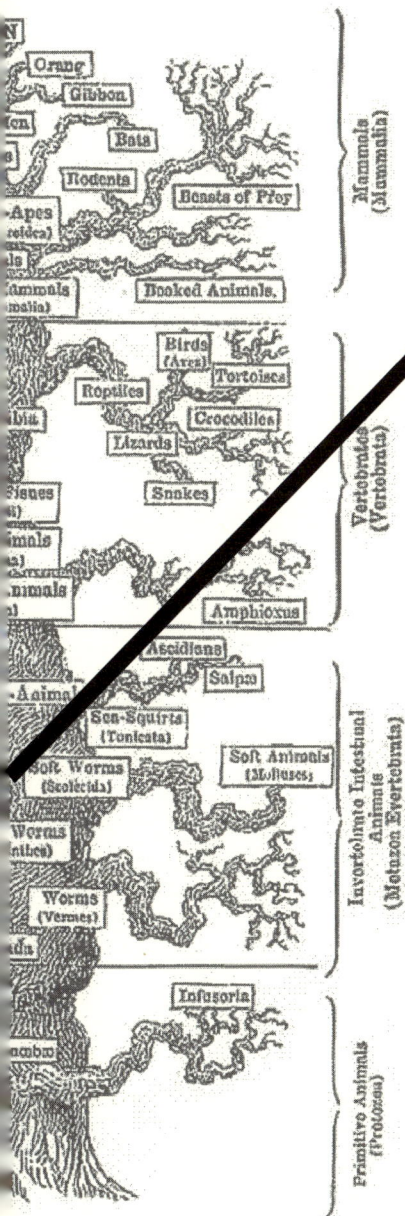

even of cosmic scale. In attempting
this, I was interested in a poetry
that might accomplish what Celmins
does in her work—inducing a
sense of our cosmic anonymity as
an enactment of a kind of post-
Enlightenment absorption of the
individual in the ultimate communal.

The Bush of Life
But to return to more tangible issues
of Earthly being, I'll recount one
more episode from my haphazard career
on the edges of science. For a few
years I worked with paleontologists
at the American Museum of Natural
History on the renovation of their
dinosaur halls. At the time, they
were all obsessed with a new
method of diagramming evolutionary
relationships that discarded the
"tree" metaphor—with its hierarchy
of branches from bottom upward
and implication of progress, and,
of course, "man" at the top—and
replaced it with a "bush" of ramifying
branches in which humans are located

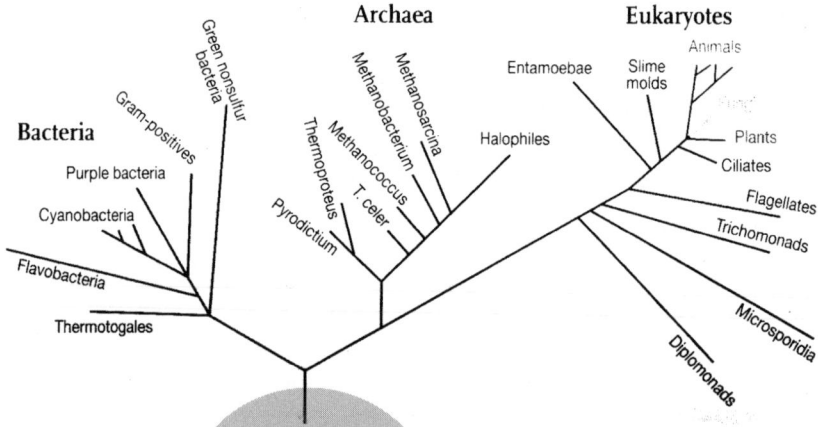

Green nonsulfur bacteria

Gram-positives

Bacteria

Purple bacteria

Cyanobacteria

Flavobacteria

Thermotogales

Archaea

Thermoproteus

Methanobacterium

Methanococcus

Methanosarcina

Pyrodictium

T. celer

Halophiles

Eukaryotes

Entamoebae

Slime molds

Animals

Fungi

Plants

Ciliates

Flagellates

Trichomonads

Microsporidia

Diplomonads

on just another twig in the thicket.
Diagramming relationships in this
format emphasizes the diversification
of life over time, but with no
notion of direction or progression.

This inspired me to try constructing
an evolutionary diagram of Feminist
Vulcanism. The diagram remains in a
very rudimentary stage, but so far
I have located the investigatory
horticulturalist Eve, the psycho-
pharmacologist Alice, and Pandora
(she-who-opens-what-others-say-
must-stay-closed), along with a
few others among its branches. As
for the common ancestor of them
all—always a subject of heated debate
among the evolutionary scientists—I
thought that might be Athena, whose
birth, at least in the alternative
version of the story, took place
after Zeus, afraid of having a child
stronger than himself, swallowed his
pregnant wife *Metis*, only to have

?

Pandora

Alice

Mina

Gertrude

Eve

Emily

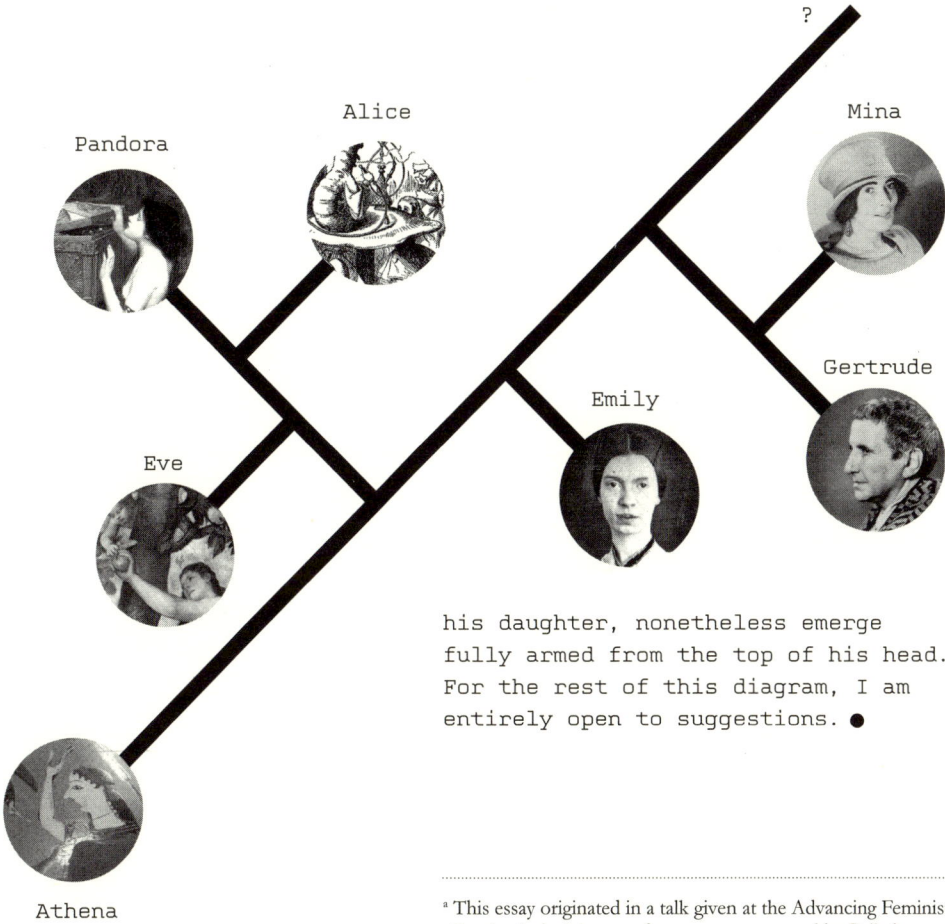

his daughter, nonetheless emerge
fully armed from the top of his head.
For the rest of this diagram, I am
entirely open to suggestions. ●

Athena

[a] This essay originated in a talk given at the Advancing Feminist
Poetics & Activism conference, co-sponsored by Belladonna
and the Graduate Center of the City University of New York,
2009.

[b] Arnold Kemp, *Art Journal*, Fall, 2001.

[c] Created by humans as a class of servants, the Cylons rebel
and destroy the Earth in a nuclear holocaust. The Battlestar
Galactica was one of a small number of spaceships carrying
human refugees. The series at first presented Cylons as soulless
machines intent on conquering space and wiping out humanity,
but eventually raised questions about the possible bigotry of
this point of view.

[d] Susan Howe, *My Emily Dickinson,* New Directions, 2007.
Emphasis added by author.

[e] I believe I first came upon this phrase in *This Compost: Ecological
Imperatives in American Poetry*, by Jed Rasula, 2002.

Opposite

15 Evolutionary diagram
of the major groups
of living organisms

Note: Special thanks to Matthew McNerney for his visual design of this essay.

JOHN KEENE

Supposium Score

BEYOND DEFAULT GEOMETRIES OF ATTENTION

Assembled after SUPPOSIUM 2014 Thought Experimenters and Participants

To suppose is to choose   A D A M P E N D L E T O N

For one or multiple people, assembled in a common space, minimum of one, no maximum

Choose one of any five paths (exile, language, philosophy, simulation, painting) on score from 0" to x" (and back to 0"/xx" if desired)

One person, one path; two people, two paths; five people, five paths; seven people, five paths, divided into differing amounts per path; fifteen people, three per path; one hundred people, divide up per path as needed; etc.

Mark out time based on suggested time quantum and length of path

Select one of the verbal phrases associated with your path or all of them, begin by stating the phrase and proceed either through repetition of the phrase, any of them, all of them, or prepared text, or improvised disquisition, poem, rap based on path concept or idea

Proceed according to score (speech, song/hum or Sprechstimme, silence, whisper)

Performers may remain stationary or move from center point outward, and back once second choral pause has been reached and performed reverse path to center

Performers may walk, dance, crawl, or simply proceed as they see fit

At first choral pause (--) use voice or other instrument for one minute sustained note

Proceed according to score (speech, song/hum or Sprechstimme, silence, whisper) until second choral pause (--), at which point participants should use voice or other instrument for one minute sustained note, followed by end of performance, or reverse of path back to start

Once performers have reached start, end in silence, or repeat process, along same path or by shifting to different path, and perform, until designated end points, or exhaustion, or infinitely

SUPPOSIUM

Speech ──────
Song/Hum ∿∿∿∿
Silence ▭
Whisper //////////

├──────┤
Time quantum
(2-5 minutes
or to be de-
termined by
performers)

- - - -
Choral pause,
break or
ending
(voice or
other instru-
ment)

Drawing
© John Keene

PAINTING

EXILE

LANGUAGE

PHILOSOPHY

SIMULATION

If they don't feel pain like we do
If body is always deep but deeper
    at its surface
If faces are not what you interrogate
If you instead reach the edge of
    the thinkable, which leaks

What does it mean to
destroy 65 years of exile?
Tabula rasa
To build or not to build
    a roof
If you have a form of life in
    the land you own it
How we activate archi-
tecture differently

During his fall he felt
    weightless
Spaceship earth
Problems with this level of
    totalizing
To what extent have we
    surrendered our ways
    of knowing to the
    power of simu-
    lated systems?

Where difference
and pleasure
meet, as practice
Fugitivity, in the
    seam
Suppose we practice
    how to listen
To conceptualize
    philosophy in light
    of the practice
    of music

To suppose is to
    choose
Multiple layers of call
    and response
We who believe in freedom cannot
    rest until it comes
A continual present of
    Black English/AAVE
Recreate the rules

x" 0" xx"

S'posin'

Suppose a non-state of mind solution to West Bank camps dead-ending in another called David meant settlers stopped reading the bible like a developer's blueprint.

Suppose citizens at the center of our thinking erased sixty-five years of roofless exile, uprising and reprisal, funerals of flag-draped caskets.

Suppose Muhammad never ascended from Al Aqsa's rock and the wailing ceased at Solomon's wall.

Suppose Jesus wasn't born at Bethlehem and his death just one poor innocent's tortured end at that dark evangel hour.

Suppose the Vatican refused to euphemize rapists as *bad apples* bounced parish to predatory parish by bishops tending their rotten orchards and the pope led his cardinals on a penitential procession through the streets of Rome.

Suppose instead of overthinking self-centric geometries we focused on centrifugal visions like Paris's poorer banlieus blurring by on the périphérique before the taxi delivers us to the capital's well-fed heart.

Suppose favelas, so picturesque from Ipanema where the reek of sewage doesn't reach and the drawn gun goes off unheard by the surf, weren't terraced into vistas for the rich by some Brazilian Baron Haussmann.

Suppose the poor weren't forced into suburban slums, "Cities of God" where maids who make the beds, Antonio who pours the coffee, board the bus before the sun is up on Guanabara Bay.

Suppose chains of what if what if what if lead to falling weightless down star-wells where time and metonymy vanish and Thales offers Pascal a pansy for his thoughts.

Suppose Diotima duets with Sarah Vaughan on *S'posin' I should fall in love with you,* Teiresias grooving on drums.

Suppose the symposium explodes, uninvited guests with names like Trayvon showing up at Agathon's door—*just kickin' it*—and we sing with Ella: *We who believe in freedom cannot rest* until even the dead take their place at the banquet.

Spectator, Participant, Audience, Actor

NOVA BENWAY: SUPPOSIUM 2014 was an exercise in collaborative public thinking—in responding spontaneously to propositions from others. I recently saw a performance of yours that involved a partnership with another dancer, as well as solicited contributions from the audience. What does collaborating in this way generate for you? Did your past experience of working in this way impact your reaction to the supposium? How do you think about "response" in your work?

LAUREN BAKST: In the performance you're referencing, I ask members of the audience to read from a two-part script with roles for "me" and "you." Because of the nature of the script, I repeatedly ask members of the audience: Do you want to be me or do you want to be you? It's important that my work acknowledges the implicit participation that comes with spectatorship. In this piece, I'm trying to set up a situation that not only acknowledges the energetic response of the audience, but also activates and unsettles our relationships to one another. I'm inviting the possibility for unknown, or less normative, modes of relating to emerge. Or perhaps just pointing to the range of confusion and desire, the constant negotiations, that live within all of our interactions. I like to let these tensions rise to the surface, and I've found that with this particular structure, it's really playful and pleasurable for me. I also like this structure because it asks people to make a decision.

As a dancer, my training was essentially an immersion in "collaborative public thinking." I have a lot of practice making instantaneous and improvisational decisions within the context of a group and trying out all kinds of embodied social relations. So when I find myself in a situation like the supposium, I'm for the most part comforted. Within the context of a lecture, it is easy enough to disengage or feel on the outside. The facilitation of response puts some accountability on the part of the listener. And I think it is through these kinds of responsive encounters that ideas can really move through people and into the world.

Because my work is performance-based, I'm always sensing the response of the audience at the moment a piece is unfolding. This interplay is not quantifiable, but it is felt. How do you experience or facilitate response through your work as a curator? I'm also curious about the remnants of the supposium—what has stuck with you? How does your own work relate not just to the content of the supposium, but to the way it organized "collaborative public thinking"?

BENWAY: I'm glad you brought up something I suspected about dance (but could not know from experience): the immediacy of response to the audience. It seems that the dance relies on and is made with the audience, who, as partners, are enthusiastic and reticent by turns. It is interesting to think of the supposium in this way—as an experience that was entirely composed, like a piece of music with an irregular cadence: the audience/participants sat quietly taking notes for the first half, then there was a flurry of dialogue—during which, significantly, my group wavered between wanting to come to agreement and wholly rejecting that possibility—until we ran out of time, and had to simply DO something, for an audience (i.e., perform). I know you use recordings and brief, pop-length songs in your dances—do you ever cut things short, or run out of time? That is what struck me most about the event: the fact that we ran out of time. We did not come to any "satisfactory" conclusion; we simply ended and went home. That is another reason why I thought it would be appropriate to discuss it with you: it seems there is a strong relationship between this kind of group dialogue and contemporary dance or theater, where one confronts a composition without a conclusive structure. A lot of curatorial projects that interest me, including the program at the Drawing Center here in New York that I co-curated and you participated in, make time for exchange between artists. Open Sessions explores the process by which something is "finished"—when do we present or display a piece? When does a dialogue become an idea, and get "produced"? I think that looking at the different ways that potential becomes "real" could have a political valence, as it addresses the question of how we move between idealism and pragmatism. And I think that too often, artists are encouraged to ignore that process and just present complete and polished work.

BAKST: This notion of an inconclusive structure really resonates with me—it's how I want the theater to feel. It speaks so directly to Sandi Hilal's "thought experiment" from the supposium. The closed plaza she described, which has four walls and no roof, is an intentionally unresolved space. One must choose to enter the plaza, to walk through the door, and therefore accept responsibility for participating in the space, while at the same time surrendering to the openness of the structure—the instability or lack of control it points to.

It's helpful to think of the supposium as another kind of, albeit very different, composed and inconclusive encounter. I remember leaving with this strong desire to continue the conversation. I also wanted more time, wanted to figure something out, or to feel some kind of satisfaction. The exercise of jotting down, jumbling up, and rearranging the speaker's phrases lent itself to these free-associative, instinctual, aleatory responses. After all of the groups presented, it felt as if all these sentiments were left hanging in the air. And so the question becomes, now what? In my work/life, I'm constantly negotiating a similar balance—the desire to figure something out (whatever that means), and the act of waiting, of letting ideas float in the air for a while, of bathing in them. This has everything to do with time—and the play between doing something or letting a structure/experience *do* something to you. Both are necessary and important processes, and I think they actually support each other. You brought up this idea of the process by which something is "finished." I'm interested in how the "doing something," which for me means performance, can still be in this unfinished finishing process. The work I'm making now feels very much like a web or a puzzle. Each iteration reveals a new configuration of the pieces. This thing you brought up of how potential becomes "real" feels totally crazy for me. I'm like, does that happen?! How? I mean, I guess it happens all the time, but

I think I tend to be consumed by the space of potential as the "real"... I don't think I answered your question. Do I ever run out of time or cut things short? Hm. I *try* to listen to time. Usually it tells me when to keep going or when to let go.

BENWAY: Interesting that you raise the question of how "doing something"—performance or otherwise—can retain an unfinished quality. How do you think about commitment in this context? Is commitment—to a set of practices, an idea, a partner—a useful term for you? Potential has a bad reputation; it's seen as a cop-out, a deferral of commitment. The two terms are often placed in opposition to each other. But as a curator, I almost always work in dialogue with an artist: we decide the parameters of a project together. I commit myself to that situation, binding myself to both the project and person at once. I appreciate the confusion this creates, the impossibility of anticipating or controlling the outcome. I like to think working this way maintains the equilibrium between potential and commitment. It draws attention to the balance required to negotiate our decisions.

BAKST: It's funny you should bring up commitment. I'm actually an extremely commitment-oriented person. I find myself working with the same materials and people and parameters for years. When I talk about the space of potential being the space of the "real," I'm referencing my own practice as a maker, which is kind of like committing to a practice of undoing and rebuilding. The current project I am working on is made of memory, echo, and trace. It is constantly invoking and producing new remainders, new ghosts. So in a way, the piece is never finished. It is not on a path to production. But it is also active and committed. It is cared for and caring. It is a thing but it will never be whole. Dance is also very much a part of this approach because it is a form where the imaginary meets the materiality of the body, and also where, simultaneously, it is possible to move within and against the materiality of social structures. You could say it is both potential becoming real / real becoming potential.

JOAN RETALLACK: Thank you for inviting me into your conversation. After thinking about your comments on running out of time, and about commitment, I offer two faux koans:

> JOHN CAGE: You know, we always have all the time in the world.
> JR: Commitment is making something constructive out of what is actually happening.

One thing that actually happened during the supposium was that we—despite our structural intentions—ran out of time. The plan was for thirty or more minutes of conversation after the group performances of "Swerved," before dispersing into post-Supposium space-time. We hadn't counted on so many audience-participants (of course, a wonderful surprise) so everything took longer than anticipated. Neither did we realize the museum's inability to grant us extra time in the room.

There are things I like about running out of time. The moment we "run out of time" we are—conceptually, but also psychologically—thrown into a dimension of palpable timelessness. Defying Einsteinian physics—a timeless zone is static space. Many metaphors no longer apply: the flow has stopped. The ticking has stopped. Prior intentions disappear. All alarms signaling "time's up" go silent. There's an explosion of silence because sound requires time. Uncollected fragments of notated space (the cards from our game) hang suspended in a metaphysical vacuum. Is this not the perfect setting for Cage's redirection of attention? An opportunity for noticing what was previously inaudible, invisible? We run out of time and the centrifugal force of all that remains restive, unresolved, unglued becomes an exploded diagram of dispersed parts (see fig. X), new configuration for new ways of seeing, new geometries of attention. What then?

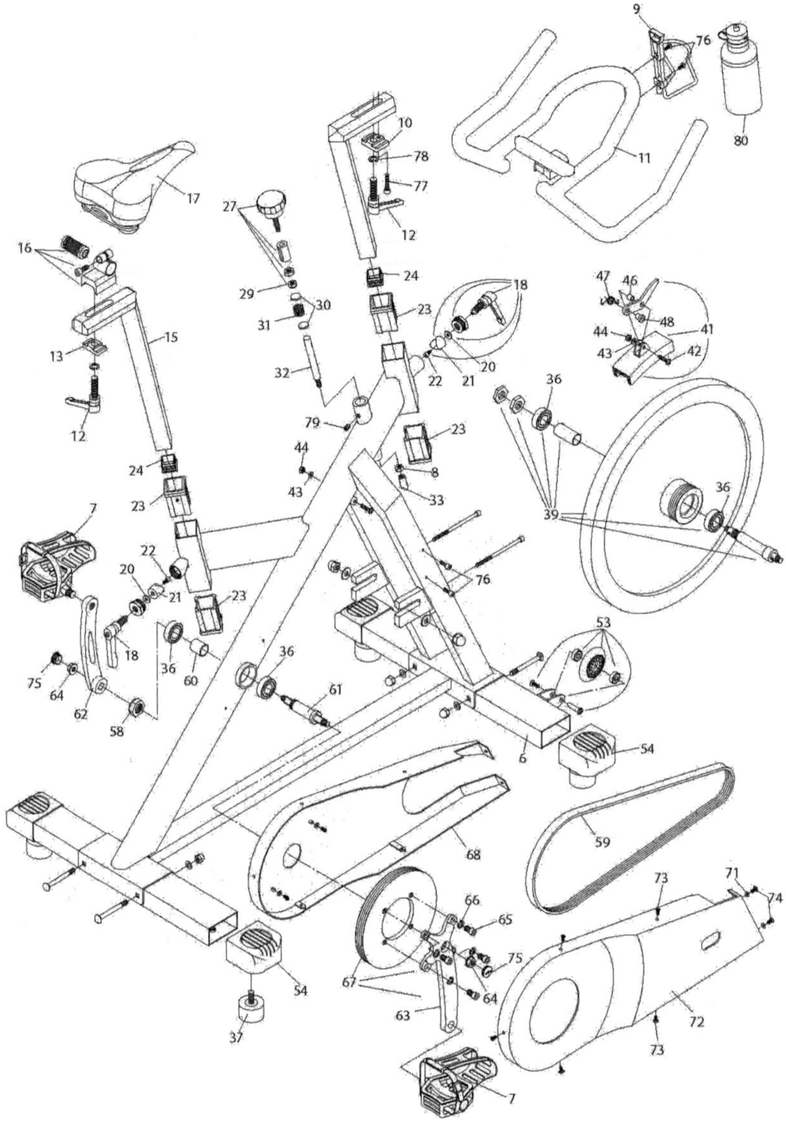

FIG. X. EXPLODED DIAGRAM OF STATIONARY BIKE

BENWAY: Is it possible for me to "agree" with Joan's koans? They certainly strike me as meaningful in terms of my experience of the supposium. They follow the logic of performance as much as of discourse. I have wanted my contribution to this text to articulate my part in the supposium, during which I played the role of spectator and participant, audience and actor, all at once.

BAKST: It is exciting to think about the space that's created when we run out of time. Can we linger in this space? Are we doing that now? The supposium asked that we redirect our *geometries* of attention. Maybe this has to do with a reprioritizing—a shift away from time and its anxiety, and a move towards space. Space creates an invitation for action.

ALHENA KATSOF

Incantations

AUTHOR'S NOTE

In the days that followed the supposium, I prepared a small contribution for Openaries, a project organized by the artists Laura Aldridge and Anna Mayer. They created a portable ceramics kiln out of oil barrels, which was temporarily installed in three distinct locations across the city of Glasgow. Aldridge and Mayer invited artists to participate in a themed firing event at each site. With words from the supposium rolling around in my head, I assembled these three incantations—one for each firing—which were read aloud at the start of each event.

INCANTATION I

An incantation for Thought forms / Theories of the universe (uttered rather than written) / John Baldessari

Calling Adam Pendleton:

Aural oral body
Language that occupies
Language occupies
I cannot sleep
I cannot rest

INCANTATION II

An incantation for Vaginas and snakes

Calling Anne Carson:
If she begged
If she came to the table
If the sentence doesn't matter
If body is always deep but deep is at its surface

INCANTATION III

An incantation for ever open openings / Ever more open openings / The expanded vessel

Calling Fred Moten:

Supposition of fright.
[30 seconds of silence—don't say anything]
Suppose I'm not supposing—I'm in love with you
Our thing would be subordinated and we would have to keep falling in love with that
Suppose I'm not supposing.

MÓNICA DE LA TORRE

A Theory of Reception

"What is a hole?" a clown asked his partner in a ring at the Circus
Medrano. Having thus confused the fellow, he wasted no time in
lording it over him: *"a hole,"* he said, *"is an absence surrounded by
presence."* […] Indeed, to be a good pataphysician, one would have to
be simultaneously a poet: and what I mean by that is someone who
creates what he is talking about the very moment he is talking about it.
RENÉ DAUMAL, "THE PATAPHYSICS OF GHOSTS"

Enter not enter.
Start there.
Out of tune.
Disturb.
Notes as valuables—
hidden so well
their location is forgotten.
A breeze stirs the woods.
Redirects foliage,
if only temporarily.
[Weather <u>erasure return</u>.]
Insights you're prone to make a note of—
you'd had them already
but they'd escaped your attention.
As opposed to butterflies.
Reconsider.

If barely formulated intuitions
cling onto another's phrasings.
This instead of that.
Trade off or parallax?
A rich braid.
A doubling, tripling, and so on.
Practice over practice.
Leaks.
If nothing sticks.
Stand ground.
Use mock knowledge.
A counter-diction.
Another's jottings swerved.
Cascade compl …
It means what?
Branching
Necessarily forward.
On going until time runs out.
Feed back. *
Followed by 50 blank pages.

JAMES SHERRY

The Poetic Argument*

> I have often thought how interesting a magazine paper might be written
> by any author who would—that is to say, who could—detail, step by
> step, the processes by which any one of his compositions attained its
> ultimate point of completion.... Most writers ... would positively
> shudder at letting the public take a peep behind the scenes....
>
> EDGAR ALLEN POE

Conventional Aristotelian argument aims to make a point and is usually divided into
two parts: the writer's stated position / proposition / assertion / story and examples
or citations as proof. This is the structure of academic writing, journalism, scientific
writing and legal briefs. From the environmental perspective, however, the real
"proof" regarding any system lies not only in its logic and authoritative concurrence,
but also in its effective assimilation into the reader's mind and the current culture as
well as its sustainability. Hence things that make no sense whatsoever and receive the
disapprobation of all the specialists continue to thrive. *Trying to stick to the point of
structure, / I'm tired of shifting from one foot to the other / without winding forward. /
Nevertheless, one path is hard / to distinguish from another, / so let us begin.* "A significant
idea of organization cannot be obtained in a world in which everything is necessary
and nothing is contingent" (Wiener 1964, 322).

A more comprehensive validation of complex issues would emphasize the interactions
between the components of essays that are as essential to survival as membranes
between beings, i.e., the interface of their ecology. To represent these connections,

---

* What follows are excerpts from a longer essay in progress.

"The Poetic Argument" suggests a third component (italicized) in each paragraph of the essay: what the writer is actually thinking about beyond the constraint of argument. *You can tell when you're onto something because so many doubts immediately occur. If the middle component were simply wrong, it would be easy to dismiss and link to fewer objections. If it were feasible, why not consider it, even though the argument then totters?* "In our view, the value of complexity concepts is at a metalevel, in that they suggest new ways to think about problems and new questions that should be posed and answered, rather than specific concrete steps that should be taken as a result" (Ramalingam et al. 2008, ix).

This middle component can speak to conflicts or ambivalence about the argument that I'm making, an emotional response to the reasonable trajectory of the argument, another kind of consciousness, a conscience, a tangent, an example from another part of the forest, a complaint, a swerve in thought, thinking in action. The middle component makes it possible for the citation to address either the argument, the middle section or both in a way that an aside in a footnote cannot. It can move away from the discourse and style of the rest of the document or stay with it. The middle section has as many options as any writing can conjure. This middle section could be many and/or distributed, but I choose it to be one. It's also a way to reference many other kinds of ideas together, since adding a third component substantially increases the relevant permutations, references and associations. *As a poet, I'm interested in how to increase comprehension with form, since form carries meaning more easily and with greater diversity than explanation.* "Form is power; because being a promise of good, it recommendeth men to the favour of women and strangers" (Hobbes 1651, 54).

Aligning the components of the essay in this way replicates the diversity of the biosphere by including individuals and their consciousness. While it is neither unique nor new to break with conventional essay writing, the possibility of adding other relevant discourses in the middle of one discourse is both biomorphic (endosymbiosis) and relevant to the essay form. *One way to be many, many integrated into one, one as many, many now one and many: my body, my desserts, my will, my divisions, what's to come. Freedom within formal constraints.* "By philology, I mean the science of everything that depends on human volition: for example, all histories of the languages, customs, and deeds of various peoples in both war and peace" (Vico 2001, 5).

Cultural assumptions, psychological underpinnings and alternatives to the argument of the essay appear together in the middle section of each paragraph and refer to the varieties of connective tissue extending beyond the main line of reasoning. The argument connects to prior discussions in the field; the citations connect to the argument; the middle section emphasizes the connectors—right, left, center, bidirectional connections, unidirectional connections, continuous, discontinuous, fast, slow, strong, weak—that may contradict or support the writer and argument, various points of view associated with the argument or simply what this particular point raises for me unbidden. *Rumination, reverb, reflection! I am happy to be me, but I'm sure that's not all I am. Limits asunder, limits dilate, diverse causes, obscure effects: an aesthetic or swerve from bias toward actual. This principle of poetry frees us from ourselves without subsuming us in the group. The fight to be me now won, I may simultaneously become my parts.* "It is erotic when parts / exceed their scale" (Hejinian 1992, 33).

Some postmodern essays, starting with Nietzsche, take the liberty of extending literary style in a non-Aristotelian manner, thereby undermining and providing an alternative to nonfiction writing's formal, scientific, legal or methodological rigor. But often the personal style of the loosely organized postmodern critical essay in some ways reduces the possibilities further by focusing even more intently on the individual writer/style: commoditized free form. Postmodern essays often go to absurd lengths to make the essay allusive, indirect, oblique or suggestive while retaining a consistent style emanating from oneself, sourcing oneself while retaining the whole (holistic) self as stylist. Is the individual under attack? Where is the world? *Do not writers validate their thoughts with form? Is not life, as Anne Tardos says, "defending a form"? What is the difference between nature and freedom?* "If it is in fact a question, in connection with the creative functions that the signifier exercises on the signified, of speaking about it in a worthwhile way, namely not simply of speaking about the word but to speak, as one might say, with the grain of the word, to evoke its very functions, perhaps the subsequent teaching this year will show you that there are internal necessities of style, conciseness for example, allusiveness, even some sting…. [These] are perhaps the essential, decisive elements necessary to enter a field of which they control not only the avenues, but the whole texture" (Lacan 1957, 21).

In fact, even in a conventional academic paper, citations point to networks of publication and provenance, an ecosystem of ideas and claims. If one constructs an argument, that argument is generally indebted or opposed to other arguments. Footnotes often discuss corollaries or objections to an argument and make digressions which might approximate what the writer is actually thinking? This variety of approaches still revolves around the argument/citation dichotomy of organism/ world. Such papers are forever attacked by another argument that sticks to its point like an individual organism protecting itself. All writing, particularly under arbitrary constraints, is biomorphic. Argument is perpetuated, word warfare among war protestors. If we reject autocracy, we must replace oversimplified methods of validation in art, science and social science. The tactic in this essay is speculative, designed to raise the issue of how to present new approaches to complex problems. In the form of this essay, the varieties of materials are collected in each paragraph as if the paragraph were an organism rather than an ecosystem to the extent that they are separable. *All these changes just make things less comprehensible; just stick to the tried and true. Don't think so much. Think from your gut, act directly. If only I could have one view of the world that elevates me, but each refers to another moment of looking at one another.* "The general conclusion I would reach is that the term *Lebensform* works in the direction of destroying the dualism language-world but, contrary to the opinion in Hurley, the practice is something always embedded with the form, with rules and norms—even the so-called rules of thumb or practical norms—because we could only speak of life when our actions can be judged by the other components of our community" (Biancini 2009, 57).

JAMES SHERRY • 113

THE PROGRESSION OF THESE THOUGHTS
THROUGH THE STUTTERING OF THEIR FORM

These three aspiring components—a logical, an indeterminate, a citational—match the impetus toward multiplicity in environmental poetics. Each paragraph sketches the form of an organism. In this way, the three components also question the difference between the individual organism and multiple organisms/paragraphs grouped into ecosystems, societies and essays. They also confront individual style to expose it as a rhetoric of self. *Of course, these components should cluster with their own ideas and nomenclature to promote them. But when alternatives appear, how long will they fight for their preconceptions as the water rises? Even after Trump's election progressive factions insist on their nomenclature of identity politics when all alternatives to mainstream religion, politics, race and gender are all equally threatened. To be fair, a common speech takes time to develop.* "The mechanisms underlying cognitive-dissonance reduction in human adults may have originated both developmentally and evolutionarily earlier than previously thought" (Egan, Santos, Bloom 2007).

A note on method: It was difficult to manage the logic and what I'm actually thinking about together, so to be sure I got a result where each of the three components made sense itself, as a group, as well as in paragraphs, I extracted the three components into columns, edited them separately and then replaced them into paragraphs. *Delusion makes sense and, of all the* things *I've said of form, I most want to say what form does, the pain and injustice caused by forms such as this, what drove writers toward free form and I, now, to re-form.* "In aesthetic forms, cruelty becomes imagination: Something is excised from the living, from the body of language, from tones, from visual experience. The purer the form and the higher the autonomy of the works, the more cruel they are. Appeals for more humane art, for conformity to those who are its virtual public, regularly dilute the quality and weaken the law of form. What art in the broadest sense works with, it oppresses: This is the ritual of the domination of nature that lives on in play" (Adorno 1997, 50).

The essay here questions whether humans are suited for long-term survival or whether our evolutionary inheritance, based on solving short-term problems, inhibits us from complex strategic thinking. For example, America's penchant for freedom of action and fulfilment of individual desire prevents us from understanding our collective impact on the planet. Our species' proclivity for oversimplified, binary thinking creates false dualisms. Some conditions, however, seem to be inherently dualistic. The binary we notice first is that every organism differentiates itself from all else; it's vital to survival. Many two-part structures reinforce this creature binary such as two eyes, two hands, two parents, night and day. Humans tend to extrapolate in the way our organismic binary replicates itself throughout our thoughts and actions. Stimulated by the primary dualities of individual organisms, cultures echo the physical world with us and them, mine and yours, leader and follower, healthy and diseased, good and bad, grammatical and ungrammatical, poetry and prose even though none of their boundaries are impermeable.... *What starts as impulse, a biological fact that I see in the mirror, ends as defended space, a fortress of ego.* "The proto-self can place on the organism a sense of 'ownership' with respect to its actions, thoughts, and mental states" (Vicari 2001, 151).

Social life, the creatures that inhabit it and the things they do to each other function with simple dual codes. *It's not all about Mommy and Daddy. Sometimes they let me crawl into bed between them.* "Thus it is an internal premise for the system's own operations constituted within the system when the latter uses the difference of self-reference and other-reference ('internal' and 'external') to order its own operations" (Luhmann 1989, 22).

After seeing a couple of horses, few children mistake them for cows. After reading a couple of poems, few readers mistake poetry for journalism or political science. How do such inferential suppositions inhibit comprehending complex realities? *Talk about sustainable. Our individual worldviews are formed early and mostly beyond our control. Inferring many from few, there's too much poetry; there's not enough poetry; there's exactly the right amount of poetry; poetry does (not) have values/meaning/progress/2,3,4.* "We build rich causal models, make strong generalizations, and construct powerful abstractions, whereas the input data are sparse, noisy and ambiguous" (Tenenbaum et al. 2011).

Rimbaud colors vowels and somehow the reader understands. *I was eating colors under the sea to stretch across electoral optics.* "Golfes d'ombre" (Rimbaud 1871)!

Surrealist juxtaposition provokes boundless content. *Logical conclusions, on the other hand, escape us. The poet works!* "…when functioning normally the mind still seems to obey none other than those suggestions which rise from that deep night I am commending" (Breton 1924).

Chance operations evoke sense through a simple model. *The world operates in probabilistic ranges, why can't poetry?* "I can't understand why people are frightened of new ideas. I'm frightened of the old ones" (Cage 1988, 212).

Language writing exploits multiple significances to invoke its dual agenda of politics and prosodic (nonlexical) meaning. *"I hate speech" politicizes the referent and marginalizes the concerns of a questionable voice emanating beyond the text itself.* "… polysemous, at once horrific and tenderly ecstatic and whatever else" (Perelman 2003)?

In each of these examples, poetry takes us away from our assumptions and proposes alternative readings of reality. *Can poetry alter our view of nature?* "The lusty stealth of nature" (Shakespeare 1606).

To be continued…

BIBLIOGRAPHY

Adorno, Theodor. *Aesthetic Theory*. Translated by Robert Hullot-Kentor. London: Continuum, 1997.

Biancini, Pierluigi. "Language as Environment: an Ecological Approach to Wittgenstein's Form of Life." In *Language and World: Papers of the 32nd International Wittgenstein Symposium, August 9-15, 2009, Volume XVII*, edited by Munz, Puhl, Wang. Vienna: Austrian Ludwig Wittgenstein Society, 2009.

Breton, Andre. "Surrealist Manifesto." 1924.

Cage, John. *Conversing with Cage*. Edited by Richard Kostelanetz. New York: Psychology Press, 1988.

Egan, Louisa C., Laurie R. Santos, and Paul Bloom. "The Origins of Cognitive Dissonance." *Psychological Science* 18, no. 11 (2007).

Hejinian, Lyn. *The Cell*. Los Angeles: Sun and Moon, 1992.

Hobbes, Thomas. *Leviathan or Matter, Form, & Power*. London: Andrew Crook, 1651.

Lacan, Jacques. *The Seminar of Jacques Lacan / Book V / the Formation of the Unconscious / 1957-1958*. Translated by Cormac Gallagher from unedited French typescripts. London: Karnac, 1957–1958.

Luhmann, Niklas. *Ecological Communication*. Translated by John Bednarz. Oxford: Polity Press, 1989.

Perelman, Bob. "This Just In: Past Haunts *Lip Service*." *Jacket 22*, 2003.

Ramalingam, Ben, et al. "Exploring the Science of Complexity: Ideas and Implications for Development and Humanitarian Efforts." London: Overseas Development Institute, 2008.

Rimbaud, Arthur. "Voyelles." 1871.

Shakespeare, William. *King Lear*. Act 1, scene 2. 1606.

Tenenbaum, Joshua B., et al. "How to Grow a Mind: Statistics, Structure, and Abstraction." *Science* 331, no. 1279 (March 11, 2011).

Vicari, Giuseppi. *Beyond Conceptual Dualism*. Amsterdam: Editions Rodopi, 2001.

Vico, Giambattista. *New Science*. London: Penguin, 2001.

Wiener, Norbert. *I Am a Mathematician*. Cambridge: MIT Press, 1964.

ERICA KAUFMAN

Que(e)rying Our Classroom(s)

SUPPOSE A VOCABULARY

One semester I had a class that was silent. I'd had other silent classes, but this one was particularly determined to resist speech. Each day I'd begin by asking someone to share something from their reading journals. Silence. I'd ask someone else to share. Silence.

I resist the word "queer," particularly the idea of a "queer pedagogy." Queer, in its adjectival form, feels too volatile for me to use because of the danger of its obscuring the myriad complex identities one might encounter in a classroom setting. Is it the case that each time I enter a classroom I queer it, am queering it, because of my own body? Am I always engaged or engaging in a queer pedagogy because of how I identify? Does one have to be legibly (or visibly) *queer* in order to queer the/a classroom space? What is the difference between "queering" a classroom and practicing a critical pedagogy committed to social justice and change? Is "queering" the/a classroom really all that *queer*?

In her "Foreword" to *Tendencies*, Eve Kosofksy Sedgwick reminds us that "queer is a continuing moment, movement, motive—recurrent, eddying, *troublant*. The word 'queer' itself means across—it comes from the Indo-European root *-twerkw*, which also yields the German *quer* (transverse), Latin *torquere* (to twist), English *athwart*" (xii). In "Queer and Now," Sedgwick continues to complicate the various "things that 'queer' can refer to: the open mesh of possibilities, gaps, overlaps, dissonances and resonances, lapses and excesses of meaning when the constituent elements of anyone's gender, of anyone's sexuality aren't made (or can't be made) to signify monolithicall" (8).

How does one reach across a silence? How do you invite the possibilities of speech? After several weeks of grappling with these questions I began to wonder what would happen if I left the room? Was my own body the problem? It was hard for me to imagine how I might be stifling the voices of fifteen first-year college students, particularly in a class of interdisciplinary First-Year Seminar readings where I was no more an expert than they were. When the endless silences occurred, we were reading Plato's *Republic*. I wondered what would happen if I left the room.

We had gathered at our usual time, around the usual seminar table, the wooden arms of our chairs covered in student graffiti. And, I asked my usual questions—*Who wants to start us off? Would anyone like to share from your reading logs? What questions do you want to bring to the table?* Silence. *I'm going to step out of the room for a while. This isn't meant to be punitive, I'm just tired of listening to my own voice and I worry that if I keep sitting at this table my voice will continue to fill the space. I know you all have things to say that I want to hear. So, I'm leaving. I'll just be in the hallway, but I want to suggest that you see this as an opportunity to talk to each other about the text. Talk, ask questions, look at passages, read out loud.*

I stood in the hallway for at least fifteen minutes and could hear the conversation. The group talked about justice, about the figure of Socrates, about what it means to engage in dialogue(s). I returned to my seat. Silence. I turned my chair around, back facing the group. After a few minutes of uncomfortable giggling, conversation resumed. And, ironically, the conversation was about the workings (or purpose) of a city-state (society). The group talked about how groups work and why.

Someone began to write on the board. I turned my chair around and rejoined the table. No one noticed so I stayed silent and just listened. We got through the first two books of the *Republic*. Ten minutes before the end of the session I asked the group to do some reflective (or process) writing—*What did you notice about today's class? What happened today that we want to make sure to learn from and perhaps replicate?*

One student voiced anxiety about what it means to speak in the context of a college classroom, particularly as a woman. Another student worried about being wrong, sounding "dumb." No one said anything directly about the role of the professor in all of this—the comments focused on their own insecurities as first-year students, new to the college, and new to each other. Instead of focusing on myself as the problem, my own physical presence as teacher, I began to think about interventions one can make on the historically normative space of the classroom.

I resist the word queer, resist the idea of a queer pedagogy, the idea(l) that the classroom is a space to be queered. Sedgwick reminds us: "A word so fraught as 'queer' is—fraught with so many social and personal histories of exclusion, violence, defiance, excitement—never can only denote; nor even can it only connote; a part of its experimental force as a speech act is the way in which it dramatizes locutionary position itself. Anyone's use of 'queer' about themselves means differently from their use of it about someone else" (9). I resist "queer" in the context of pedagogy because it is simultaneously too broad, too blanketing, and too complex. I think of my classroom as a space of querying, shifting a place to take risks, be transient, sometimes deviant, and creative. To query is to question, doubt, act, ask, unsettle, to remain skeptical of correctness, to suppose. To query is itself a queer act because it pushes one to take risks, to think beyond what is known, to enter into uncomfortable territory.

SUPPOSE A QUERYING

Joan Retallack's opening remarks for SUPPOSIUM 2014: Beyond Default Geometries of Attention offered the following framing question: "since default modes of thinking tend to remain fixed if undisturbed, and since most of us find it unpleasant to be disturbed, suppose there were a form of proliferating interaction (something like a game) designed to increase the number of playful inter-disturbances among us. Would that increase chances of unsettling our default modes of thought, opening up new geometries of attention?" This question resonates with the way I approach any classroom I enter—what "default modes of thought" already exist? What interventions might be useful to create "proliferating interaction," to shift student-teacher dynamics so that an authentic learning community evolves?

The terms "queer" and "query" are both central to composition and rhetoric, a field that focuses on questions of how and why we teach, questions of literacy and power, with particular emphasis on writing and the required first-year writing course. Despite my discipline's emphasis on the classroom and the *how* of teaching, much of the theoretical work published is just that … theoretical. I'm always interested in the lived, the lived experience, "the continuous present." When a word like "queer" enters into the discipline, it becomes another blanket term, another label to affix to what we likely already do. Instead of imagining the real-time of the classroom and what one might do to create a safe, inclusive, interactive, democratic/anarchic space, much of the literature focuses on teaching texts about sexuality or on coming out in the classroom.

In "Towards a Queer Pedagogy of Conflicted Practice" (2008), Mary Armstrong suggests:

> Like queer itself, queer pedagogical practices are hard to define—and, of course, in many ways that is the point.... Queer pedagogy demands we think hard about what makes the queer classroom queer, as well as what we wish to achieve when we try to imagine about queer positive educational spaces: What is the queer classroom? Who and what are these queer students, teachers, materials and ideas? What effects do we hope queer pedagogy will have on students, instructors, and institutions?

To Armstrong's list of questions I would add: How do we create inclusive classrooms without making any assumptions about who the students are/will be? How can one begin to locate a pedagogical space between the form of teaching and the identity of teacher/student? What do we do with power? How can one genuinely "practice what they preach"—locating a balance between practice and praxis, theory and reality?

SUPPOSE A SPACE FOR LEARNING

Karen Kopelson concludes "Rhetoric on the Edge of Cunning" (2003) with a central pedagogical question: "*How* might we speak, *as whom* might we speak, *so that students listen?*" The answers to these questions remind me of Amy Winans's (2006) idea that "a queer pedagogy draws attention to the parameters of questioning, thus highlighting the process of normalization as it draws attention to the places where thinking stops." In other words, when the act of questioning becomes a collective act, one in which the question is always in question, the result is a kind of dialogue in which normalization is examined rather than accepted. If we question the full

ERICA KAUFMAN • 121

spectrum of rationales behind the way we use language in the classroom, attention is drawn to "the parameters of questioning," and by doing this, students listen because they participate in the content being generated.

In November 2016, more than halfway through the semester, I found myself returning to Kopelson's questions as a way to prepare myself for class.[1] "*How* might we speak, *as whom* might we speak, *so that students listen?*" From the outset of the semester it was impossible to ignore the ideological weight of the charged election campaigns, particularly given the fact that, while Bard College is a liberal arts institution, it is also situated in rural upstate New York. As the election date grew closer, the tension between our surrounding communities and the campus increased, and difference and discriminatory events proliferated, including several incidents involving conflict between students and "locals." It would have been just as conspicuous to leave the political climate unacknowledged in the classroom, as it would have been to make my own opinion or identity explicit to students.

After reading, discussing, and writing in response to works by Plato, Shakespeare, Rousseau, and John Stuart Mill, on the morning of November 9, I prepared to tackle *Democracy in America* by Alexis de Tocqueville (1835) with my students. It would be literally impossible to continue to contain direct conversation around the idea of American democracy. Daunted by the already tense dynamics of the group, a tension rooted in the potential volatility of its obvious but unspoken spectrum of political views, I felt stymied—could I really engage Tocqueville's views of democracy and maintain a classroom space that was inclusive and nonjudgmental? How could we attend to the text at hand while refraining from assumptions about the politics of the individuals in the room and the way these students felt in the aftermath of the election, the first election any of them voted in?

I knew that the pedagogy I'd relied on up to this point would no longer suffice. It wasn't that I had to leave behind the ritual of beginning with writing and ending with writing and lots of conversation in between. It was that I needed to figure out a

---

1   In the fall semester I teach a writing-intensive great-books survey course required of all freshmen. The overarching question that framed this particular semester (as decided by the course's co-chairs) was "what is political freedom?"

way to exert more control, to direct or hold our dialogue in a way that I usually don't. I found myself wondering how to subvert my privilege as the "teacher" in order to invite us to explore other ways to be together. I needed to figure out how to deploy my professorial authority without behaving in a way that ran counter to my own ethos of how I approach the classroom—ideally, the way I exert my "authority" is to create a space of respect and collaboration and then get out of the way. I suppose this might be considered a kind of "queer pedagogy" in the way that I am always querying my own position as teacher and the hierarchies at play in institutional spaces. But, is this "queer" or part of my own personal pedagogical ethos, an ethos committed to seeking out what is overlooked, uncomfortable, and outside the "norm"?

On November 10, 2016 at 4:40pm we convened as usual. We sat around the seminar table. We did a few minutes of private free writing. I then invited the group to write down the following: (1) One question for yourself; (2) One question for people who do not share your views; and (3) One question that is not yours alone, but for the community (or communities) you belong to. We took some time responding to these questions in silence in our notebooks.[2] After about ten minutes, I invited us to share any of these questions—the constraint was that there would be no talking or oral response to the questions. We were just going to put them into the atmosphere of the classroom.

I then suggested we revise the way we approached our response journals—reading logs we'd kept all semester as a record of our thinking about the texts we were studying. The new questions I offered were: (1) What is the text saying about _____? (Pick one central idea in the text to write about.) Respond without making interventions based on current events. This is an exercise in close reading. Look to the text. And/or (2) Does this have any relevance to what's going on now? Given our contemporary situation, what can (or should) we learn from this text? I let the class know the changes I was suggesting were a way to stay grounded in our texts.

Democracy in America begins with an "Author's Introduction," which I'd assigned as our sole focus for that day, imagining that we'd spend the class session engaged

---

2   These questions came out of a conversation with a colleague, Nicole Wallack, about the role (or potential) low-stakes writing holds in the aftermath of a big event.

in collaborative close reading. The first sentence reads: "Amongst the novel objects that attracted my attention during my stay in the United States, nothing struck me more forcibly than the general equality of conditions." Many of the questions we'd shared from our writing spoke to issues and concerns regarding "equality"; however, the equality we were referring to was specific to 2017. Tocqueville's text was written as a direct response to what he'd observed on his visit to America in 1831–1832. In his introduction to the abridged edition of *Democracy in America*, Michael Kammen contextualizes Tocqueville's response as "deeply influenced by the cultural baggage he brought from his native France; an abiding fear of political instability and the repeated denial of individual liberty there…. Hence, the immense appeal of what appeared to him, in contrast, to be the remarkable presence of political stability, individual freedom … " (1). Needless to say, America to a Frenchman in 1831 looked very different from the America we see as Americans today. How much contextual knowledge about France in the early 1830s would students have? And, how could this even be at the forefront of their minds in the aftermath of such an election?

SUPPOSE A THEORY

I've been writing this version of this essay over and over again since November. I suppose I'm trying to figure out why something about working with this group of students on Tocqueville led me to fixate on the phrase "queer pedagogy." What does it mean to label a practice "queer"? What provokes this desire to identify any action as such? I can't resist my impulse to query into "queer," but I also can't articulate what is driving this interest in a term I say I don't want to use. I'm struck by Kevin Kumashiro's "Queer Ideals in Education" (2003) and how he looks at the relationship between queer activism and social-justice education. He writes, "Queerness is not a natural state of being. Rather, queerness is produced as a contrast, as that against which normalcy is established" (367). Does a queer pedagogy foster an ethos that exists fully in contrast to normative classroom procedures? How is this way of being in a learning space different (queerer) than anti-oppressive pedagogy and/or radical pedagogies?

SUPPOSE A QUERYING

In "Diversity and Inclusion: Toward a Curriculum for Human Beings" (1993), Maxine Greene builds on John Dewey's idea that democracy is "a community always in the making." Greene continues, "educators may begin creating the kinds of situations where, at the very least, students will begin telling the stories of what they are seeking, what they know and might not yet know, exchanges stories with others grounded in other landscapes, at once bringing something into being that is in-between" (218). In previous classes, even previous silent classes, the exchange of writing and stories is something I knew/know how to provoke. But, what happens when there is an obstruction preventing any exchange between individuals, particularly those involving not knowing? How do we create conversation when the act of sharing any form of language seems so beyond what the bodies in the room are able to deploy?

The week after the election, our second class on *Democracy in America*, we began by going around the seminar table, each sharing a few sentences from our reading logs. Our goal was to listen carefully and actively, ultimately working together to generate a list of "key words" that were repeated across logs when writing about Tocqueville. These words included: "freedom, equality, liberty, tyranny of the majority, democracy, republic, and individualism." After listing these terms on the board, I suddenly found myself self-conscious about how heavy-handed I was being—any conversation we were having was heavily controlled (by me) and rooted deeply in the text and nothing else. This is the opposite of what I'd hoped for—a class in which the students learn to listen to each other and do more than simply talk and react. How does one reach *across* a silence? How does one welcome noise?

After generating our list of somewhat predictable "key words," I then offered the following questions to the group: According to Tocqueville: (1) What is democracy and what does it entail? (2) What dangers does democracy pose for political freedom? and (3) What dangers does democracy pose for intellectual freedom? I crafted these questions ahead of time, but presented them as if they'd come out of the reading logs and words we'd shared. What I didn't know was how to take these questions and create a conversation in a space where even reading out loud felt forced. I normally look to questions, to the act of inquiring, as a way to twist, shift, or even thwart dialogue in an effort to push ourselves to some new curiosity or question. In an essay on John Cage, Gordana Crnković focuses on the role of questions and questioning on chance operations. She writes, "the language of questions is the language of self-alteration through interaction with material practices" (183).

"Self-alteration" and "interaction" are terms I associate with "queerness," words that skirt normalcy (or complacency), queering or querying what's at stake in the language we use to communicate with and for ourselves. By posing my three questions, I hoped to ground us in the text, while disrupting our silence, but I also knew that this could not happen through ordinary discussion. Earlier in the semester, while reading Plato's *The Last Days of Socrates*, we created and attempted to perform our own Socratic dialogues. I don't remember this working particularly well, but what I do remember is the pattern of speech that the format evoked. Someone would pose a question, someone would offer a hypothesis followed by a new question, someone would restate and perhaps revise the prior hypothesis, also adding a new question, and so on. In that context, the dialogues resembled the cross-examination that Socrates often seems to engage in, twisting his interlocutor's claims until he reaches some answer regarding their validity. In his attempt to tease out differing opinions, in his desire for debate, can the Socratic dialogue be considered a queer process? Is there something to be gained by thinking about this act of querying as queer?

The Socratic Seminar is often used (particularly in secondary schools) as a way to teach critical thinking—students learn how to ask rigorous questions, engage claims, and practice the art of persuasion. Given that the group was already familiar with the Socratic dialogue, I decided to use the questions I'd posed as a frame for a series of Socratic Seminars. We divided the class into three groups, each group received one question, and spent the remainder of that class period in their groups generating constellations of questions linked to the larger question they were assigned. The groups also noted down moments in Tocqueville that connected with or complicated the questions they drafted. Some groups worked silently, each individual crafting their own roster of queries. Other groups generated their questions collectively, with one designated note-taker keeping track of the conversation. The groups were created randomly, by counting off—this felt like an important way to begin to diminish my own thumbprint. Additionally, the Socratic Seminar is a structure without a leader;

the goal is to engage in rigorous conversation without depending on a teacher or power figure to keep watch.

In "Queer and Nondemagogic Pedagogy in the Classroom," Robert Faunce (2013) suggests that a queer pedagogy "seeks to interrogate the heteronormative, and encourage disenfranchised and marginalized voices" (31). Faunce goes on to investigate the ways that a queer pedagogy is useful "as a developing tool for all voices … it is a way of refracting the structural power back upon itself by working within its framework, rather than rebelling against it" (32). Instead of stressing the bodies the word "queer" includes, Faunce proposes a queer pedagogy that begins by learning how structures of power work, then subverting and querying them. Confronting *Democracy in America* with and without italics began to seem to be an opportune time to try to actually parse what Tocqueville saw and why he decided to transcribe his trip in the way that he did. Similarly, I wondered if there was a way to step out of our contemporary moment and use the palpable tension in the post-election classroom as a way to query the way "structures of power" influence our interactions in the classroom. I wanted my students to do more than question norms, I wondered if there might be a way to see the classroom as a space where the contrast that is queerness might become visible through critical thinking.

SUPPOSE A SEMINAR TURNED QUEER

I did not give specific directives.

I did not use the term "Socratic Seminar."

I did not participate in a group.

Instead, I suggested: "Think about questions that might facilitate *moves*—we want to try to push our thinking into new terrain!"

I did not check in on the three groups. I felt uncomfortable.

I worried about the groups.

I worried about the groups again.

Ten minutes before the end of class we all reconvened to do some writing. *What does it mean to ask a good question? Can the act of inquiring help us to notice anything new about democracy?* We did not share these.

SUPPOSE A QUE(E)RYING

Still the week after the election, our third class on *Democracy in America*, we began with a few minutes of private free writing, followed by five minutes to check in with our groups and review our writing on the process. I introduced the day's work by suggesting that we use the questions we'd generated in our groups and spend our time asking questions instead of talking. Each group had twenty to thirty minutes to facilitate and the goal was to start with the assigned question and then lead the group in a conversation by honoring each person's comments and offering questions to push the conversation forward. Here are some snippets of our seminars from my own notebook:

1: "What is democracy and what does it entail?"
2: "I think that democracy for Tocqueville has to do with equality and individual freedom—on page thirty-seven he even refers to it as the *spread of conditions of equality*."
3: "Thank you. I definitely think that freedom and equality are important terms for Tocqueville. I do wonder if he understands these words in the same way that we do now?"
4: "Great question. I think that it is impossible for someone from France writing in 1835 to have the same definition of freedom as we do now. But, does that even matter?"

The goal was for each "seminar" to actually come to a natural close—the groups continued to pose questions until there was a prolonged silence. We would then clap, pause to take stock of our thinking in writing, and then move on to the next group.

John Dewey referred to *Democracy in America* in order to propose: "popular government has at least created public spirit even if its success in informing that spirit has not been great" (207). I'm interested in Dewey's use of "public spirit" because of how it describes the kind of atmosphere I was hoping to find—a space that could hold difference so that a community of listeners could begin to form. A space focused not on political affect or invisibility, but rather on developing ways to find critical approaches for the histories and perspectives that we did not want to obscure. Querying and writing together, focused on a shared text, allowed for political subjects to co-exist in the classroom, and I was struck by how structured discussion practices created a safe space but not a sterile one.

I suppose this sounds idyllic and even utopian.

I suppose it might sound as though the class transformed and we all joined together in celebration of conversation—sitting around a seminar table engaged in lively and respectful dialogue.

I suppose it might sound as though the tensions of the semester melted away and we became a nurturing community. However, I've only described three class sessions and my focus on these three is because they signify the moment I saw challenging dynamics begin to change.

I suppose the emphasis here should be on *begin*. The class *began* to change; challenging dynamics began to shift.

In order for this to happen, I had to interrogate these dynamics, thoroughly plan these class sessions so that I could actually step away.

I had to trust what I knew about this particular group of students—that they would do the reading. Even if silent and tense, I knew that this was a cohort that showed up fully prepared.

I had to resist the urge to directly acknowledge the political tension alive in the room, only tacitly acknowledging it by saying that we were going to work differently together.

I had to believe that we could work differently, and that the way we would do this would be through actually embarking upon the kind of work I'd planned.

I had to accept that the students might not have any reaction to the new plan, to the idea of sharing in continuous student-led seminar conversations. But, that each student in the room spoke at least once meant the change I wanted had begun.

BIBLIOGRAPHY

Armstrong, Mary. "Towards a Queer Pedagogy of Conflicted Practice." *Modern Language Studies* 27, no. 2 (2008): 86–99.

Dewey, John. *The Public and Its Problems*. New York, NY, Henry Holt & Company, 1927.

Faunce, Robert. "Queer and Nondemagogic Pedagogy in the Classroom." *The CEA Forum* (2013): 30–44.

Greene, Maxine. "Diversity and Inclusion: Toward a Curriculum for Human Beings." *Teachers College Record* 95, no. 2 (1993): 211–221.

Kopelson, Karen. "Rhetoric on the Edge of Cunning; Or, the Performance of Neutrality (Re)Considered as a Composition Pedagogy for Student Resistance." *College Composition and Communication* 55, no. 1 (Sept. 2003): 115–146.

Kumashiro, Kevin. "Queer Ideals in Education." *Journal of Homosexuality* 45, no. 2–4 (2003): 365-367.

Perloff, Marjorie, and Charles Junkerman, editors. *John Cage: Composed in America*. Chicago: The University of Chicago Press, 1995.

Plato. *Plato: Republic*. Trans. G.M.A Grube. London: Hackett, 1992.

Sedgwick, Eve Kosofsky. *Tendencies*. Durham, Duke University Press, 1993.

Tocqueville, Alexis de. *Democracy in America*. Edited by Michael Kammen. Translated by Elizabeth Rawlings. Boston: Bedford/St Martins, 2009.

Winans, Amy E. "Queering Pedagogy in the English Classroom: Engaging with the Places Where Thinking Stops." *Pedagogy: Critical Approaches to Teaching Literature, Language, Composition, and Culture* 6, no. 1 (2006): 103–122.

IV

SUPPOSIUM 2014, DOCUMENTATION

Preliminaries[1]

As part of his 2013–14 residency at MoMA, Adam Pendleton commissioned Joan Retallack to conceive an event or installation of some kind to be proposed to the curatorial staff and—if approved—presented in some part of the MoMA complex. (The invitation was *that* open.) The rules of Pendleton's residency prohibited public announcement of any events he commissioned. Hence, the participant audience was invited from a list assembled by Retallack, Pendleton, and MoMA curators.

---

1   Some of the documentation in this section is minimally edited for clarification. For example, the original letter to Sandi Hilal assumed her knowledge not only of the location of Al Quds University, but of its collaborative partnership with Bard College.

INVITATION TO A FEATURED
THOUGHT EXPERIMENTER

January 10, 2014

FROM: Joan Retallack, Annandale-on-Hudson, NY, USA
TO: Sandi Hilal, Beit Sahour, West Bank, Palestine

Dear Sandi,

I am a poet and professor at Bard College, and have been working with faculty at Al Quds Bard in Abu Dis, West Bank for some time. I'm currently helping to develop an Arabic Language & Thinking Program for the entire university.

I've been following and immensely admiring your work with Alessandro Petti on DAAR (Decolonizing Architecture Art Residency). Recently, on YouTube, I saw a four-part interview in which you explained how your design process for a plaza in a [Palestinian] refugee camp involved reconceptualizing the subjectivities of refugees through a series of conversations with members of the community. I was very interested in the way your process was, in effect, a cluster of interrogative thought experiments conducted via conversation.

I would very much like to show some portions of these interviews during an event I'm organizing at MoMA, NYC, March 2, 3pm–6:30pm. I'm calling it SUPPOSIUM 2014 in both homage and departure from Plato's *Symposium* on love. There will be five featured speakers, each of whom will introduce a thought experiment (beginning with "suppose") in tangential relation to the very fuzzy and unwieldy topic of our current global situation—a kind of mega-Emergency of too many emergencies. Your explanation of DAAR and your work on designing the improbable (from the point of view of conventional assumptions) plaza for a refugee camp will bring an important (culturally and materially specific) contribution to the event's conversation.

I find your interviews illuminating and moving in their implications for reconfiguring geometries of attention in seemingly "much too complex" crisis contexts. I'll be meeting with Audio Visual technicians at MoMA next week to discuss how best to screen material from outside the room. I want to find out whether we can set up a good Skype link as well. If we can, I wonder if you might be willing to join us via Skype in order to introduce a thought experiment of current interest to you. I would love to bring that kind of portal to Palestine into the collective consciousness of the room. I'm attaching one of several descriptions of the SUPPOSIUM, including one that highlights the connection to John Cage's redefinition of silence. There happens to be a Cage exhibit in the museum which will still be up in March.

With best regards,
Joan

EDITOR'S NOTE

Instead of screening excerpts from the YouTube interview, we were able to show a video that Sandi Hilal prepared specifically for SUPPOSIUM 2014. The transcript of her talk about the process of designing the Fawaar refugee camp plaza was our opening thought experiment (see page 3). We were not able to arrange a Skype connection.

SUPPOSIUM 2014
Beyond Default Geometries of Attention
[Six Thought Experiments Beginning with *Suppose*]
Sunday, March 2, 3–6:00pm
Founders Room, MoMA

In the midst of our planetary emergency of too many emergencies we will enter a space-time bracket of serious play / playful gravitas initiated by a series of six bold thought experiments beginning with "Suppose … "

You are invited to join our featured speakers in a collaborative engagement concluding with conversational procedures—puzzling and conjecture—whose results will appear, along with the thought experiments, in a book titled *The Supposium*—an updating and irreverently respectful homage to *The Symposium*, Plato's poetic exploration of *erōs*.

ANNE CARSON
Poet / Classicist

SANDI HILAL
Architect; Co-founder, DAAR—Decolonizing
Architecture Art Residency, a West Bank project

PETER KRAPP
Author, *Déjà vu: Aberrations of Cultural Memory;*
Noise Channels: Glitch & Error in Digital Culture

FRED MOTEN
Cultural Critic / Poet; Author, *In The Break: The*
Aesthetics Of The Black Radical Tradition

ADAM PENDLETON
Artist; Author, *Black Dada*

JOAN RETALLACK
Poet-Essayist; Author, *The Poethical Wager*

Limited Seating
RSVP: supposium@moma.org
To Reserve a Place

THE JOHN CAGE CONNECTION

It happened that an exhibition titled *There Will Never Be Silence: Scoring John Cage's 4'33"*—curated by David Platzker—was up at MoMA before, during, and after SUPPOSIUM 2014, from October 12, 2013 to June 22, 2014. There would be many cross-resonances. We sent the following note to everyone who RSVP'd.

SUPPOSIUM 2014
Beyond Default Geometries of Attention

The most significant thing John Cage did after stepping out of the anechoic chamber at Harvard in 1951 was to challenge the legacy of an ancient understanding of silence. Rather than absence of sound (impossible), Cage redefined silence as sound/ noise we're not noticing. By extension, this pertains to everything escaping the scope of our awareness: pleasures, hazards, negligence, brutality, surprises of every kind, improbabilities, possibilities. Cage in effect invited us to notice and redirect our geometries of attention.

Why is this crucial not only to artists who have from the outset benefited from the Cagean redefinition of silence but to all concerned with our limitations in addressing the proliferation of large-scale crises on our planet? Each seemingly demanding full attention with, it seems, not enough attention to go around.

That is a framing question of the MoMA supposium (somewhat edgy homage to Plato's dialogue—*The Symposium*, on the nature of love). Our conversation will begin with a series of thought experiments posed by featured speakers and will then proliferate throughout the room to be worked on collaboratively. The procedural structure of the entire event is conceived as an experiment (playful and grave) in negotiating conjectural complexity and issues of scale as we attempt to think constructively about contemporary predicaments and possibilities raised in the talks. A primary challenge will be somehow taking them all into account.

An underlying puzzle is whether we are capable of reinventing or at least redirecting our geometries of attention as well as the poetics of our discourses in ways that enable intersubjective conversations across our many interpersonal alterities and divergent interests. What imaginative constructs are required to work productively (together) on the emergency of too many emergencies?

Aftermath: Talks by initial speakers and samples of what we construct in conversation (language, ideas, models) will be published in a book titled *The Supposium*.

The Event

JOAN RETALLACK'S OPENING REMARKS

I want to start by acknowledging the remarkable gathering of people in this room, and particularly Adam Pendleton who set the idea of this supposium ticking in my mind over a year ago when he invited me to propose a project that his MoMA Residency might sponsor. I also want to thank all the MoMA curators who were supportive, even enthusiastic, about an idea that was, and remains, intentionally indeterminate with respect to its outcome.

The procedural rational, however, is not hazy. It has to do with strategies for eluding default geometries of attention, as the *we* in this room, along with the planetary *we*, face the great emergency of a cascade of emergencies generated and sustained by many of those default modes. One of my thought experiments in conceiving this event (which is itself a thought experiment in action) takes the form of a compound question: since default modes of thinking tend to remain fixed if undisturbed, and since most of us find it unpleasant to be disturbed, suppose there were a form of proliferating interaction (something like a game) designed to increase the number of playful (even pleasurable) inter-disturbances among us? Would that increase chances of unsettling our default modes of thought, opening up new geometries of attention?

Since you have now populated this room with a substantial number of potentially playful mind-bodies, any and all of which have the capacity to constructively disturb one another, we are collectively in a position to try this out.

Before explaining the equipment and procedures for our work, I want to say something about the part of the supposium's conceptual framework connected to John Cage.

This is fortuitously relevant because of the exhibition, *There Will Never Be Silence: Scoring John Cage's 4'33"* which is up in the museum until June 22.[2]

The most significant thing John Cage did after stepping out of the anechoic chamber at Harvard in 1951 was to challenge the legacy of an ancient understanding of silence. Rather than thinking of it as an absence of sound (impossible), Cage redefined silence as sound/noise we're not noticing. By extension, this pertains to anything escaping the scope of our awareness, implicating all our senses. By pointing this out and enacting it in his compositions, Cage in effect invited us to both notice *and redirect* our geometries of attention and, thereby, to notice things previously obscured in our cultural silences.

Why is this crucial not only to artists who have from the outset benefited from the Cagean redefinition of silence but to all concerned with our limitations in addressing the proliferation of large-scale crises on our planet? Each one seemingly demanding full attention with, it seems, not enough attention to go around. This is a framing question and active challenge for our interactions in this supposium (somewhat edgy homage to Plato's dialogue—*The Symposium*—on the nature of love). Our conversation will begin with a series of thought experiments posed by the featured speakers, and then will proliferate throughout the room in procedural collaboration. The procedural structure of the entire event is conceived as an experiment (playful and grave) in negotiating conjectural complexity and issues of scale as we attempt to think constructively about contemporary predicaments and possibilities raised in the invited talks, and brought to this gathering by everyone else in the room. Can we somehow manage to take more than we normally imagine possible into account? As Cage would say, "we don't know but we can try."

An underlying puzzle is whether we are capable of reinventing or at least redirecting our geometries of attention, as well as the poethics of our discourses, in ways that

---

2 The next three paragraphs are a slightly revised version of the "John Cage Connection" emailed to the RSVP list.

enable conversations across our interpersonal alterities, divergent interests, and values. What imaginative constructs are required to work productively (together) on this contemporary emergency of too many emergencies?

You've each been issued a Supposium "kit": 4"x6" spiral-bound pad—either red, yellow, or blue; pen; five index cards; and an instruction sheet for the card game we will play after our mid-supposium refreshment break. To prepare for our activity in the second half of the supposium, try to listen to our series of thought experiments with heightened attention—not only to the ideas expressed but to the language that composes them. Your pad is for noting down words and phrases that strike you as you listen. After each thought experiment there will be a two-minute silence for you to write responses and questions. By the time we take our symposium-inspired food and drink break we will have material for everybody's active participation in Supposium, part II.

The way the quasi-logical set of thought experiments to follow have to do with geometries of attention can be exemplified as follows: One familiar geometry of attention is the relation of center to periphery, where center is object of focus, periphery becomes fuzzier and fuzzier, tending toward ultimate invisibility the farther it extends. In most—if not all—cultures the center is reserved for what is valued most highly; the periphery becomes a hodgepodge of what is least valued. These value discrepancies affect everything, everyone as they determine the nature of cultural attention—from socio-politics to the arts. The "fortunate" center tends to habitually, strategically ignore the outliers, while to a great extent constructing its self-definition by what it excludes. On an international level, the raison d'être of nation-states is to create and defend the material representations and values of its center. Stateless and occupied peoples, exiles, refugees, the chronically impoverished, the racially and ethnically besieged, women in any of these categories inhabit peripheries whose horizons—from the perspective of the center—mark nothing but vanishing points. Peripheral invisibility can be built into landscapes as border walls, built into consciousness by intentionally discriminatory or oblivious habits of mind.

Sandi Hilal, our first presenter (by video from one of those peripheries: the West Bank, Palestine) is an architect and cofounder of Decolonizing Architecture Art Residency—DAAR. She is also a UN consultant on conditions in refugee camps in the Palestinian territories. Her thought experiment has to do with reversals of geometries of attention, including the implications of situating refugees at the center rather than at the peripheries where it has always been assumed they belong. Because Sandi is the only presenter who could not be physically with us—could not fully participate in the ongoing conversation this afternoon—hers is the only presentation I've previewed in this intro. Bio information is on your kit sheet for Hilal, and our other thought experimenters: Peter Krapp, Adam Pendleton, Fred Moten, and Anne Carson. Remember to observe the two-minute intervals of silence after each talk.

A PROCEDURAL GAME OF CARDS AND PERFORMANCES

SWERVED
An (Index) Card Shuffle[3]

1. In your pads, bracket words and phrases (speakers' and your own) that most interest you in what you noted during the presentations.

2. Choose 6 brackets with language/ideas most "charged" with implications and/or puzzlement. Write them 2 per card on 3 cards without attempting to connect them. Put your initials in the top right corner of each card so you can retrieve them at end of game.

3. In your small group, read your cards to one another. (Note in your pad anything that interests you from others' cards.) When everyone has read, pass all cards to a volunteer shuffler who will deal them back to you in mixed order. If you get back more than one of your own, work out a trade so you have at least 2 cards not yours.

4. Compose a (brief) collaborative (performative) response to the featured presentations, or a new thought experiment; in either case, draw ideas and words from the language on the cards. Each of you should try as best you can to take into account the linguistic hand you've been dealt as well as the spectrum of ideas in your group, incorporating what others value not in order to form a consensus but to reflect a multiplicity of concerns. This may require embracing contradictions.

When the large group reconvenes, we will ask for presentations (readings or performances) of some of what was composed in the small groups. To be followed by open conversation.

---

3 This instruction sheet was read aloud before we moved our chairs into small group circles.

At the end of the supposium, you can leave response notes in the box at the door. For more considered responses, questions, thought experiments—whether developed from your group work, or in subsequent collaborations, or individually—you can send us the results for possible inclusion in "The Supposium," a post-event publication. Please include contact information for all authors. Contributions must be received by April 1.

Two Reviews

MÓNICA DE LA TORRE

Just in the last year or so, poetry has been appearing in other contexts outside of the ones typically provided by poetry's channels and institutions . . . [I]nstances that stand out for me are: Susan Howe's letterpress prints *Tom Tim Tot*, shown in the 2014 Whitney Biennial, as well as the inclusion of the independent publisher Semiotext(e), which participated in the biennial by commissioning booklets by twenty-eight authors, among them Ariana Reines, Dodie Bellamy, and Eileen Myles.

Even more remarkable perhaps, for it brought together communities that rarely overlap, was Adam Pendleton and Joan Retallack's SUPPOSIUM 2014: Beyond Default Geometries of Attention at MoMA this past March. [It] featured six presenters of "thought experiments beginning with the word suppose": Retallack, Pendleton (a conceptual artist and poet), poets Anne Carson and Fred Moten, the Bethlehem-based architect Sandi Hilal, and simulation-theory scholar Peter Krapp. Audience members—artists, curators, scholars, and poets—were instructed to take notes during the presentations and then break into groups. Each group literally compared notes and then collaboratively swerved them, by collaging and reinterpreting them, in order to produce a joint response. The last part of the event, in which all the responses were delivered before the attendees, was very much like an Oulipian poetry reading: because of the directives we followed, all the texts produced on the spot had almost the same language, but reconfigured differently. You could recognize a bit of Carson's poem braided with a quote of Pendleton's on black speech and a phrase of

---

4 This review is excerpted from a blog post originally published on the Poetry Foundation's *Harriet* on July 9, 2014. An earlier version appeared in *BOMB* #128, Summer 2014.

Moten's on Miles Davis, or a thought of Retallack's on John Cage's notion of noise combined with something Hilal said on the architecture of Palestinian refuge camps, for instance. The subtleties of each permutation drew your attention in a direction different to the one you'd gone in when first listening to the presenters. The irony of this happening in MoMA's Founders Room did not escape me. Did the fact that our thought experiments took place in an art museum context have any effects on their contents and efficacy? They would be swerved and reintroduced into the art world again. Months later, at Pendleton's first exhibition at Pace Gallery in Chelsea, I'd see the presenters' names silkscreened onto a few very handsome silver canvases in the back room of the gallery.

REVIEW OF MOMA'S "SUPPOSIUM" MARCH 2014[5]

DANICA SAVONICK AND LYNNE BECKENSTEIN

This March, the Museum of Modern Art hosted its first ever "Supposium," an afternoon of philosophical revelry that challenged participants to think beyond ordinary binaries—silence and sound, center and periphery—that might blind us to the extraordinary. This year's event, "SUPPOSIUM 2014: Beyond Default Geometries of Attention," featured six eclectic luminaries: Anne Carson, Sandi Hilal, Peter Krapp, Fred Moten, Adam Pendleton, and Joan Retallack. The supposium's mysterious flyer announced that "In the midst of our planetary emergency of too many emergencies, we will enter a space-time bracket of serious play / playful gravitas initiated by a series of thought experiments beginning with 'Suppose ... '" The conditions of this conditional are "emergency," invoking both the exigency of global precarity and the emergent possibilities for imagining alternatives.

Joan Retallack began by asking the audience to approach these performances in a spirit of playfulness, as though the panelists' "strategies for eluding default geometries of attention" were part of a game—a game in which we were all active participants. The premise was that, in this mode of being "playful mind-bodies with the capacity to disturb," we might unlock "the puzzle of the supposium." In other words, we might transcend certain fixed modes of thinking about large-scale global crises, while considering what constructs allow us to do that work. Rather than operating in a traditional critical mode, the event's thought experiments invited us to consider the generative role of performance in re-issuing the clarion call for Black English in the wake of Trayvon Martin and Jordan Davis and humming along with Miles Davis as (re)visionary soundscapes of democracy and justice.

---

5 This review appeared February 5, 2015 on the CUNY Academic Commons website with a "better late than never" note.

Sandi Hilal was the first to take up Retallack's challenge to destabilize our old models for determining value. She theorized the architecture of permanence and belonging through the conditions of exile in a West Bank refugee camp. Rather than privilege the political discourses of nation-states, Hilal reviewed the history of the "roofless camp" from 1948 to the present, in which Palestinian refugees refused to build structures that might imply permanent resettlement. In doing so, she raised critical question about rootedness and the right to return: How might these roofless homes help us to rethink collective spaces? How can they inform our attempts to put the refugee at the center at the world?

Peter Krapp situated this work of supposing within a long history of simulation, reviewing how the category of the thought experiment has evolved against a backdrop of political crises and technological innovations. To test the validity of our assumptions, we have to "close down the critical distance," and engage in role-play without a rigid binary between real and unreal. For example, can we make the imaginative leap required to envision data-mining on a planetary scale? How might information about global warming help us "optimize global behavior," and sync up to cool down? To fail may be expensive, though the cost of inaction is worth the risk.

Adam Pendleton began with a memory of a freestyle-rap performance, telling the story of how Common, DJ Hi-Tek, De La Soul, Talib Kweli, Biz Markie, and Pharoahe Monch improvised collaboratively, shifting pace and rhythm through "multiple levels of call and response" with transformative potential. He both recounted the experience and re-staged it for us, shifting between his own voice and that of the musicians—"Find heaven in this music and God," he called out, in a refrain—as a performance of what it means to reclaim Black English. This Black English has the potential to interrogate a culture steeped in racialized violence, a culture that permits the murders of young black men like Trayvon Martin and Jordan Davis. In the idiom of twenty-first-century U.S. political imaginaries, it is a language "that occupies, that stands ground."

Fred Moten used music to tell its own story, outside of language: without comment, he played a recording of Miles Davis for us. As the sound waned, he began to expound upon the recursive arrangement, how the jaunty sax returns to express a wistful yearning, climbing the scale with nostalgia for what has come before. Moten sang his own lyrics for Davis's melody: "Supposing I should fall in love with you," a conditional that he riffed on throughout his meditation on the social situation of philosophy. Philosophy inhabits a state of fugitivity, requiring us to "find the slave in the text," to "study how to listen" in order to speak out of turn. As in jazz, we need to understand the theme and the variation of the theme as coterminous; we get to the variation through revolt, through falling in love, through accompaniment that takes us to "the knowledge that precedes knowledge." Beyond default geographies of subject-positioning, suppositioning.

Anne Carson read her poem, "Seated Figure with Red Angle (1988) by Betty Goodwin," from her 2001 collection *Men in the Off Hours*. Before her reading, she showed us an image of Goodwin's drawing, then shared the impetus of the poem: confronted with a work of art that makes the artist want to fall silent, how does one begin to suppose? For Carson, even the grammar of the conditional was not enough to apprehend the depths of Goodwin's artwork, a sketch of a faceless figure that hovers on the surface of the page. Carson's starting point was protasis, but she left out the "then" of each "if/then" clause. In her list of seventy-three "If …" phrases, the intention, Carson said, was to leave out the fact, and leave in the hesitation: "If you reach in, if you burrow, if you risk wiping in …" Each line of the poem ends in an open-ended pause, a silence that disturbed in its refusal to finish the thought.

Following these multimodal presentations, ranging from the academic to the melodic to the ekphrastic, the audience's task was to then break into groups and respond to the presenters' injunction: "We must choose to suppose." This mode of engagement modeled a form of playful amateurism, encouraging participants to riff on the terms of the presenters' interdisciplinary fields. In our own group, we formulated and reformulated questions about power, representation, and voice, attempting to think through the conditions of exile that Hilal represented. As participants, we found ourselves uncertain about how to approach the conditions of fugitivity, refugee, and exile in the playful ethos of the supposium—that is to say, how playful we could afford to be, without occluding the gravity of these experiences? When we rejoined the rest of the audience, it turned out that most of the participants had risen to this challenge by moving back and forth between the literal and figurative, unsettling the boundary between them. They performed these responses through incantatory recitations, spoken word, and song. One group chanted pronouns and asked, "What are the pronouns conjuring?" One sang, "Language is the flight of refugees," standing in a chorus line; another broke apart to read different pieces simultaneously, facing different sections of the room.

Despite these exhilarating variations in form and content, there was a thread of continuity: the audience had latched onto the conditional and, following the example of the six presenters, now linked it to the collaborative. "Suppose there were no passengers on spaceship earth," one group suggested. "We are all crew." The supposium implicated participants in a low-stakes game, providing a playful space to experiment and fail—to figure out what works and doesn't in the poetics of dislocation. Not knowing the rules, or even what was possible, we played together for three hours in the modality described by Lauren Berlant in her series of blog posts on "The Game": "The game is a form of life coming into being, extension, and activity, the blinking open at the start of the day and the beyond to anything that was explained." Berlant offers the terms for the game in a series of conditional clauses; like Carson, she strips away the apodoses from a series of conditional statements, leaving the protases that tantalize us with their incompleteness: "If you let a piece go without completion … If we could come forth as 'I' with the other objects, if we would take in that all things don't happen for a reason …" In the silence of these unfinished "If … " clauses, we have the space to imagine different possibilities, ways of thinking for which we don't have language yet.

V

SWERVED, A PROCEDURAL POEM

FROM SUPPOSIUM 2014

Procedural Poethics

The text of our post-supposium procedural collaboration was composed from lines generated by participants during the index card game. At the event's end, approximately 200 index cards with approximately 100 participants' notations were dropped in a collection box on leaving the Founders Room. The notations were arranged verbatim in alphabetical order of first words in each of the lines written for the game. It turned out that the alphabetical procedure increased the probability that multiple lines written by any single participant would appear in different parts of the *SWERVED* composition.

SWERVED

a citizenry born of / rooted in an understanding of itself as (partially) transient . a closed plaza with four doors . a great knowledge collider . a gymnasium floor with floor filling map . a language that stands ground . a place where people will not find themselves by chance . a language where you come prepared to do something . a linguistic Buffalo . a refuge from oligarchy and a barrier to self determination and freedom . a rich braid of indirections . a roof with no walls . a valorization of shiftlessness . absence is a myth produced by spatialized language from a mode of empirical apprehension of the world . absence: distant lovers, passing seconds, missed calls, poverty/lack, the silence that is really an answer ... the spaces that turn marks into meaning . action words . action words . agency within / against language and architecture . ain't . ain't nobody sing like Tina . ain't nobody sing like Tina . ain't nobody sing like Tina . all necessary Aristophanes and contrafactual Fats Waller . all necessary data . allure v. awake . alternate . alternate evidence . Amiri Baraka line about finding out the good and the bad → knowledge of good and evil as something *desirable* (but maybe still dangerous?) . an idea of interrogation . anechoic . Aristophanes and Fats Waller – a more useable continuum . art pain . assume the apposition . audience / performer continuum . back home . Baraka / Dorn – earnestness anti-relativism . beat . behavior . beyond public / private . beyond total experience . black boxing a lot of thinking – therefore we don't know what it is. . black boxing thinking . Black English elimination of "do" (what you want?) and

"-ed" (she close the door) – does this collapse time verbally? . body implicated in thought experiment always . braid . but we must not succumb to permanent indecision (stress) . call on the body . call and response . call and response in jazz, hip-hop, blues, and gospel – all Black and American forms – why so predominant? . chains of what if what if what if . children's play = home . choose our language . closed plaza is still an open space . collective . collectively disturb . come back and tell what happened . come prepared to do something w/ language . come to my window I'll be home soon . condiment . conditional leaves hesitation intact . conditionals as either graven or "where can I write this?" – the written word as sacred, indelible, *does* something … continual present . could care (which is palpable) constitute ownership rather than money (which is abstract) . could falling into the well have been divine intervention? . counterfactual / conditional . cutting one another as we serve one another . cutting one another as we serve one another . data model role-play . decided not to settle . despite 65 years in one location and assuming a generation of lives led and completed there is a refusal of home . disturbance . double negative . dynamic systems spaceship earth National Simulation Center . electrical light . emphatic negative as positive . emphatic negative structure towards . enigmas fought to get out (of the room) . exile – home – roof less . expropriation body figure . falling . falling down a well . feedback . fell / laughed . fight to get out . find a slave in the text . find a slave in the text . find heaven in this music and god . find music in this heaven in god . find the slave in the text . find the slave in the text . freedom . from subject to person . fugitive reading . fugitivity . geometries of attention . grab a glass of marmalade on the way down . hazy cascade escape silence . he's fabulous! standard English . his words are action words . history, fact, science are all mythologies . honoring UN 194 – right to return – gets most opposition from even liberal Jews and others – they insist the only result is the end of Israel – thinking about it is subversive – the challenge requires imagination and willingness to radically transform status quo . how the rules play out . how to leave the hesitation in . how to leave the hesitation in – black boxing a lot of thinking . how to make a *tabula* that is not yet *rasa* (but will be some day) and meanwhile live in it . how to slow down your falling by 1. using silicone 2. laughing at it 3. putting it in the 2nd person . I am sorry . I do not believe in all this relative shit . I have been trying to find language for … . I have been trying to find language that occupies, language that stands ground . I have gone deep & seen images of the world as it will be . I/I, I/u, I/we, I/us, I/he-she-it, I/they . I wanna be a spaceship earth pilot! like on the cover of Herbie Hancock's *Thrust* . if as a matter of fact . if auto . If color, choice if balance . if horses never come . if I loved u I wd marry u . if I loved you . if I were really courageous I'd be a DJ . if I were really courageous I'd be a rich braid of indirections . if legs crossed and sucked back like Christ's . if nothing sticks . if nothing sticks . if police burned their hands . if red is the color of art pain . if red is the color of art pain what is art pain and is it different from quotidian pain? . if red was the color of quiche . if the center & periphery are reversed has a transvaluation of values already taken place . if they don't feel pain like we do . if you are pushing and pushing and then it begins to pull you

. if you cannot remember what words you wrote . if you choose what to undo if you have that choice . if you choose what to undo if you know how to make that choice . if you say he is just a friend then you know what I need . if you want to know things . if your life bewilders you . I'm in love . infectious diseases or financial problems . interpenetration . interpersonal alterities . [interrogation is a desire to get information that is not given freely] . is . is jazz a formula to communicate in a group? . is red the most emotive color . is the woman who laughed a warning . Isaac Asimov in a bar in NY . it is only knowledge that will bring this moral earnestness . I've lost the ability to communicate in groups IRL . jazz is an open system but how does it communicate in a group . knowledge collider . knowledge brings moral earnestness but how do we teach in a way to make people listen . knowledge collider . knowledge of things . knowledge will build moral earnestness . lack an oral jest . leaking edge of rational possibility . language that occupies . language that occupies . language that occupies and stands ground . language that stands ground . large knowledge collider . laughter . laughter when comparing standard English to Black English from audience . leaking edge . left or escaped . let's go out of turn and speak there . linguistic buffalo . linguistic buffalo . Mach o man let us be deranged and move to the edge of the thinkable which leaks in that place between falling and throwing because your words are always action words or am I speaking out of turn . macho man tell it to my heart . meaning resides in what I just mentioned . micro disturbances . Miles / Coltrane? . mocks   slave . mocks stars . most believe a simulator is not a simulation . most valued (center) least valued (periphery) . my spaceship earth is the graven place in or on which I write this . neither public (as in administered) nor private (as in owned) . new geometries of attention . no temple can be constructed unless it is put together exactly like the human body (Vitruvius) . not private / not public . not the figure of the citizen as center of our thinking . nothing sticks . now played using a mute . obligation to lecture . ½ way . open system . optimize global behavior . optimized global behavior . optimizing global behavior . people could still suppose . philosophy is slavery . planet . playful . playful interdisturbances . philosophy is fugitivity – escape from [mental] slavery . Plato's Cave / falling into a well and viewing the world through narrow opening . positions constantly in process of becoming visible . public private collectivity . pushing until it pulls you . push'n pull . rabbit hole . race . refugee . rest in freedom . return . return home . return back "home" . reverberation and melody . reverse the structure . reverse the structure without recourse to myth . revolt in our repose . rich braid of indirection . right of return to – a theme . risk bodies pain . risk collectivities thought . role play mode . ± roof (shelter) collectivities . roof less camp . roofless . roofless . roofless . roofless home . roofless house similar to Jewish sukkot – roofless structure as part of memorial of wandering . roofless refugees favelas . roofless home closed plaza . she became just as famous even though she doesn't have a name . she have closed the door . simulation . simulation of the model of the metaphorical real . Socrates and Miles … for miles and miles and miles . Socrates missed it when he formulated the idea of the Philosopher King – Moten has it right – "Social structure of philosophy" demands end of kings, the return of the commons, the fugitive as our agent, restoration of love as rigor . softly cutting one another . space inside . spirited and spiritual response . s'pose . s'pose I'm not s'posing I'm in love with you . stand your ground – the presumption of embodied ownership, the presumption of property via whiteness – ownership as defending land / territory / ideology – Blackness cannot own, cannot claim American ground style   settle . state kill Trayvon & Jordan Davis & Black people every 28 hours – may not pull the trigger but denied justice, enabled privatized anti-Black violence – we got to have language that hits back at power . subpositional love . support . support . support, support, support meaning, meaning meaning translators, translators, translate . suppose I was at an art museum . suppose I'm not supposin … suppose I'm not supposing . suppose: START strategy games at the . study how to listen . supposability . suppose to choose . suppose we cut one another while we serve each other . suppose we derange . suppose we don't take place . suppose we practice our practice . suppose we practice how to listen . suppose we study how to listen . Supposition Explosion Reversal Derange . suppositioning . tabula rasa . take my love and share it: the social value of philosophy . take over (but can't take under) . tetragrammaton golem . the center is created by the deliberate production of peripheries . the dirt . the knocking sound right before the piano . the edge of the thinkable, which leaks (out & in) . the edge of the world which leaks . the glow of computer on Fred's face while listening to jazz reminds me of Krapp's talk on simulation . the maid was also immortal and grand be of her observing, but nameless . the music before the words after the music stops . the

National Simulation Center . the "rest" (resting) is stillness, a kind of stillness, the necessity of motion, movement . the social situation of philosophy is slavery . the thick and interesting silence which follows . the tradeoff is … I'm of of time . the thought experiment and the body thinking begin w/ the pratfall . there are no passengers on Spaceship Earth; we are all crew – Marshall McLuhan . there are 100 supercomputers in this room – why not use them . they were displaced in an act of violence in violation of international rules of engagement and denied right to return in violation of law . thinking otherwise . this and (not) a plane . thought experiment – Thales' foolishness double risk without reference to mythology . thought experiments . (to suppose is) not (to choose) . thought risk . to suppose is not to choose but to hold off on choosing . to suppose is to choose which is why freedom of thought is a privilege, a necessary luxury . totalize . trade-off . tradition / virtue ethics . triangulation without strangulation . triple negatives . triple negatives . trying to find language that occupies . understand the world from perspective of the refugee . variations coterminous with theme . warning signs and escape routes . we are sitting in a circle and here there is no center and no periphery – we're essentially eight strangers to each other's backgrounds, thoughts and identities and we've come together to make sense of language and action, ideas we heard today and things we felt – we are recontextualizing ideas, responding to the constraints of time and settling into a new way of being, collectively presenting a response to supposing . we don't take place . we must choose to suppose . we need translators . we who believe in freedom . we who believe in freedom cannot rest until it comes . we who believe in freedom cannot rest until it comes . we would like to think to you . what blues do you choose . what does it mean to destroy 65 years of exile? . what if … ? . what if we would just sing when it comes to moral earnestness . what is center what is periphery . what is on the periphery of English? . what the camp?! . what work is the word "refugee" doing in the reproduction of periphery . what you think? . whatever strikes you . when is a refugee no longer a refugee? . when the symposium explodes the music before the words after the music stops . when the symposium explodes the music before the words after the music stops . when we get to horses it is ½ over . when you take my love and share it … buried in the house . where difficulty and pleasure meet . where difficulty and pleasure meet as practice . where difficulty and pleasure meet in a continual present neither public nor private . where is a place I can write this? . where that leg? . where the doors should be . why is one possible and dominant response to these conditionals if I can write them down verbatim . without a roof . words and phrases that STRIKE you . why create micro disturbances instead of creating macro disturbances? . you can fall right through the planet .

VI

Contributors

LAUREN BAKST is an artist and writer living in New York. She works in, with, and through dance, approaching the situation of performing as an object of inquiry.

LYNNE BECKENSTEIN is a doctoral candidate in English at the CUNY Graduate Center, where she writes about feminist aesthetics in contemporary literature.

NOVA BENWAY is Executive Director of Triangle Arts Association, an artist residency founded in New York in 1982 which has expanded to a worldwide network of more than forty members. She was previously a curator at The Drawing Center in New York City, where she co-directed Open Sessions, a two-year residency/exhibition hybrid program. An alumna of the Center for Curatorial Studies, Bard College, she also holds a B.A. from McGill University, Montreal.

ALLIE BISWAS was born in England and calls London home. She started her career in the research department at Tate. She has carried out interviews with artists including Wolfgang Tillmans, Rashid Johnson, Antony Gormley and Zanele Muhole. She is the co-editor of a forthcoming anthology of critical texts relating to the Black Arts Movement.

ANNE CARSON was born in Canada and teaches ancient Greek for a living.

ALAN DEVENISH is a Faculty Associate in the Institute for Writing and Thinking at Bard College and currently teaches in the Bard Prison Initiative. He has also taught literature and human rights in the Marymount Manhattan College Program at the Bedford Hills Correctional Facility and was previously Professor of English at SUNY Westchester Community College.

SANDI HILAL is an architect based in Beit Sahour, Palestine. She is currently a fellow at Bard College where she is, together with Alessandro Petti, a 2016–2017

Keith Haring fellow in Art and Activism. She is a former consultant on the camp improvement program with UNRWA (United Nations Relief and Works Agency) for Palestine refugees in the Near East. Hilal is a founding member of DAAR (Decolonizing Architecture Art Residency, www.decolonizing.ps). She is also among the founders of Campus in Camps, an experimental educational program established in Dheisheh Refugee Camp, Bethlehem (www.campusincamps.ps).

ALHENA KATSOF is a writer and organizer of exhibitions. She curated *Towards the Unknown*, an exhibition of drawings, scores, and graphic notations by the master musician Yusef Lateef (1920–2013). Her texts appear in numerous publications including *The Artist As Curator: An Anthology*, edited by Elena Filipovic (Mousse Publishing, 2017). She is a faculty member at the Center for Curatorial Studies, Bard College.

ERICA KAUFMAN is the author of *INSTANT CLASSIC* (Roof Books, 2013) and *censory impulse* (Factory School, 2009). she is also the coeditor of *NO GENDER: Reflections on the Life and Work of kari edwards* (Venn Diagram, 2009), and of *Adrienne Rich: Teaching at CUNY, 1968-1974* (Lost & Found: The CUNY Poetics Document Initiative, 2014). she works at Bard College and lives in the woods.

JOHN KEENE is the author of the novel *Annotations* (New Directions); the short fiction collection *Counternarratives* (New Directions), which received a 2016 American Book Award and a 2016 Lannan Literary Award in Fiction; the art-text collection *Seismosis* (1913 Press) with artist Christopher Stackhouse; the art-text collaboration with photographer Nicholas Muellner, *GRIND* (ITI Press); and, most recently, the chapbook *Playland* (Seven Kitchens Press). He has also published a translation of Brazilian author Hilda Hilst's novel *Letters from a Seducer* (Nightboat Books / A Bolha Editora), as well as translations of a wide variety of poetry and prose from Portuguese, French, and Spanish, and has exhibited his artwork in Brooklyn and Berlin. A longtime member of the Dark Room Writers Collective and a graduate fellow of Cave Canem, he chairs the department of African American and African Studies and also teaches English and creative writing at Rutgers University-Newark.

PETER KRAPP is a Professor of Film & Media Studies, English, and Informatics at the University of California, Irvine. In his research and teaching he pursues interests in media history, computer culture, simulations, secret communication, and games. He is the author of *Déjà Vu: Aberrations of Cultural Memory* (2004) and *Noise Channels: Glitch and Error in Digital Culture* (2011), both with University of Minnesota Press, and coeditor of *Medium Cool* (Duke University Press, 2002).

FRED MOTEN lives in New York and teaches in the Department of Performance Studies at New York University.

ADAM PENDLETON is a New York–based artist.

EVELYN REILLY has written three books that attempt to manifest a poetics of the Anthropocene: *Styrofoam* and *Apocalypso*, both published by Roof Books, and *Echolocation,* forthcoming from Roof in 2018. Her poetry and essays have been published in many journals and anthologies, including *The Arcadia Project: Postmodernism and the Pastoral*; *The &NOW Awards2: The Best Innovative Writing*; *Omniverse*; and *The Eco-language Reader*; and will be included in the forthcoming *Earth Bound: Compass Points for an Ecopoetics*, edited by Jonathan Skinner and *Big Energy Poets of the Anthropocene*, edited by Heidi Lynn Staples and Amy King.

JOAN RETALLACK, author of *Procedural Elegies / Western Civ Cont'd,* and *The Poethical Wager*, is a poet and essayist with an early background in philosophy and visual art. Her poetic practice investigates—at times procedurally enacts—intersections of poetics and sociopolitical puzzles. *Bosch Studies: Fables, Moral Tales & Other Awkward Constructions* is forthcoming from Litmus Press in 2019.

DANICA SAVONICK is a doctoral candidate in English and a Futures Initiative Fellow at the CUNY Graduate Center, where she is completing a dissertation on the reciprocal relationships between aesthetics and pedagogy in the work of feminist and antiracist authors.

INGRID SCHAFFNER, curator of Carnegie Int'l, 57th ed., 2018, is based in Pittsburgh at the Carnegie Museum of Art.

BEVERLY SEMMES is a visual artist. A recent exhibition of her work titled *Beverly Semmes: FRP* originated at the Tang Museum and traveled to the Weatherspoon Art Museum and the Faulconer Gallery. Semmes teaches fine art at Cornell University.

JAMES SHERRY is the author of twelve books of poetry and prose, most recently *Entangled Bank*, an ecosystem of poetry and prose that expands his work on climate and culture. He is the publisher of Roof Books and started the Segue Foundation, a multi-arts producer, in 1977 in New York City.

MÓNICA DE LA TORRE is the author of six books of poetry, most recently *The Happy End/All Welcome* (Ugly Duckling Presse, 2017) and *Feliz año nuevo* (2017), a volume of selected poetry translated into Spanish (Luces de Gálibo). Born and raised in Mexico City, she writes in, and translates into, Spanish and English. Publications include Triple Canopy, *Harper's*, *Poetry*, *Erizo*, and *huun: arte / pensamiento desde México*. She teaches poetry at Brown University.

Acknowledgments

"Seated Figure with Red Angle (1988) by Betty Goodwin" was originally published in the September 1999 issue of *Artforum* and also appears in *Decreation: Poetry, Essays, Opera* (Anne Carson, New York: Vintage Contemporaries, 2005). Reprinted with permission of the author.

"Black Dada" was published in *Black Dada Reader*, edited by Adam Pendleton (Verlag der Buchhandlung Walther König, 2017). Reprinted with permission of the author.

"In Conversation: *Adam Pendleton with Allie Biswas*" was originally published in the September 2016 issue of *The Brooklyn Rail*. Reprinted with permission of the authors.

"Beverly Semmes's FRP" was originally published in *The Feminist Responsibility Project: Beverly Semmes*, a catalogue accompanying the exhibition "The Feminist Responsibility Project" at Rowan University, March 29, 2011 to May 14, 2011 and reprinted on the occasion of the exhibition "Beverly Semmes: FRP," at Susan Inglett Gallery, February 6, 2017 to March 15, 2014. Reprinted with permission of the author.

Thanks

Thanks to Sandi Hilal for her photo of the completed Fawaar Refugee Camp plaza, photo courtesy of Campus in Camps. For kind permission to use "In Conversation, Adam Pendleton," thanks to Allie Biswas and the *Brooklyn Rail*. For providing the high-resolution images that made the Beverly Semmes "FRP Centerfold" possible, we extend our appreciation to Susan Inglett Gallery.

Enormous gratitude to MoMA curators Kathy Halbreich, Laura Hoptman, David Platzker, Jenny Schlenzka—and to Amy Chen—for many forms of encouragement and assistance during the more-complicated-than-anticipated organization of SUPPOSIUM 2014. Thanks also to Studio Pendleton Assistant Zak Syroka for critical problem-solving.

It has been an honor to publish the continuation and aftermath of SUPPOSIUM 2014 with Litmus Press. My appreciation for the generosity with which founding editor and director E. Tracy Grinnell has supported the many wagers that materialized into this book is immense. That gratitude extends to managing editor Emily Wang, to "point person" erica kaufman, and to designer HR Hegnauer whose visual poesis has turned a sequence of doc files into an elegantly coherent object.

—J.R.